Creative Acts

of

Healing

Creative Acts
of
Healing

after a baby dies

&

Judith van Praag

Paseo Press
Seattle WA

Published by Paseo Press, PMB# 645, 300 Queen Anne Ave.N., Seattle, Washington 98109-4599

First edition 1999.

LCCN 99–93317

van Praag, Judith

Creative Acts of Healing / Judith van Praag

Includes index.

ISBN. 0–9672677–0–6

1.Nonfiction, Memoir. 2.Bereavement —Babies —Death —Self help.

Cover design, cover art *Starlight*, and illustrations©by Judith van Praag

ATTENTION ORGANIZATIONS, SCHOOLS OF MEDICINE, MIDWIFERY, DOULAS AND CARETAKERS:

Quantity discounts are available on bulk purchases of this book.

For information, please contact Paseo Press,
PMB #645, 300 Queen Anne Ave.N., Seattle, 98109-4599

In memory of
ARIANE EIRA
and my father Jaap.

For
my mother and my husband

&

ACKNOWLEDGEMENTS

Creative Acts of Healing is a tribute to all people who bring solace, lend an ear or a hand, or give a shoulder to cry on during times of grief. I am especially thankful for the wonderful friends who may recognize themselves in composite characters in this book.

I thank Dr. Yael Danieli for suggesting I'd write this book, Dr. Csaba Hegyvary for insisting I share it with the world and Joost Elffers for his advice on how to get it out there.

I am grateful to the following readers of the manuscript, whose comments, critique and/or miracle touch were crucial to the completion of this book:
Holly Thomas (who tackled the earliest version),
Theodora Fogerty, Jan Haag, Carol Levin, Lori Mitchell,
Edith Rohde, Jo Nelson, Gary Davis,
Ellie Mathews, and Terry Clark.

Furthermore, I am indebted to
Bonny Becker, Eve Kiehm, and Joan Stamm,
members of the writers critique group, for their
unfailing support.

This Publication was made possible, in part,
by subscribers and sponsors

FOREWORD

There is elegance
In the threads of our destiny:
Simplicities of truth entwined
With the complexities of why?
When woven from the sweetness of our moments,
They become the fabric of our being.

This brief prologue, a few lines written to a friend of mine as a message for hope, captures for me the essence of Creative Acts of Healing.

Through the art form of word and imagery, Judith van Praag arouses primal emotions and gives language and being to the "unspeakable" loss of her child, ARIANE EIRA. Her longitudinal approach to the process of grief and mourning is extremely provocative. Creative Acts of Healing will be an important resource for families.

As I live with daily loss and renewal, miscarriage and delivery, death and birth, I cry with my patients and my heart falls heavy to their losses. Yet I am not the sufferer. I could only write of loss in the third person.

Judith van Praag writes in the first person, an autobiographical journal of how she and her husband endured, suffered and recovered from this most devastating of losses.

Pregnancy and newborn loss from early miscarriage, loss of multiple pregnancies, prematurity/immaturity, genetic diseases, and death at birth such as ARIANE's are more common than most are cognizant of, and we need to recognize the emotional trauma on the parents and families of these children.

As caregivers and as members of the human family we must be able to offer comfort and solace to bereaved parents of the fetus and stillborn. The first step in this process is an awareness of the impact of such a loss on our lives. Creative Acts of Healing offers such an insight.

Perinatal loss engenders communities of loss throughout the world, bonded by the common thread of mourning the death of unborn and newly- born children. Local, national and international organizations have been established to educate, counsel, support and promote awareness to the issues of these losses, but paramount to the individual's healing process is remembering. Such occurs publicly soon after the loss in the form of rituals, funerals and memorial services and continues forever through personal thoughts of what sorrow stole and of what hope remains. At times, such memories are sallow and painful, but they can be full and beautiful and contribute to eternalize the soul and spirit of our lost children. This is clearly what Judith and her husband have done. We find in this memoir no greater love for a child than their love for ARIANE.

Michael R. Berman, M.D. Clinical Professor of Obstetrics and Gynecology, Yale University School of Medicine, New Haven, Connecticut. President Hygeia Foundation for Perinatal Loss and Bereavement, Inc.

≈

Michael Berman,has been practicing obstetrics and gynecology for 26 years. In an effort to assuage the grief of his patients who experienced pregnancy and newborn loss, Dr. Berman writes original poetry of loss and hope. He has founded the Hygeia Foundation for Perinatal Loss and Bereavement whose mission is to establish international multimedia resource centers for pregnancy loss (based on his website, http://www.hygeia.org) in medically and economically under-served communities.

Dr. Berman has presented his work to University medical centers throughout the county in an effort to enhance the awareness of the issues surrounding perinatal bereavement and loss to his colleagues.

CONTENTS

INTRODUCTION

Creative Acts of Healing attests to the power of creativity and nature as a healing force, to consultation of ancient oracles as a mode of meditation to find inner peace, and to communication as an important element of the recovery process. How creativity brings relief during the grief process is illustrated by my quest to find solace through keeping a journal, writing poetry and letters, making paper, painting, drawing, crafts, sewing and needle work.

For the first three sections: Loss, Mourning and Grief, I used a dual approach: journal entries followed by retrospective pieces written five years after the loss. The narrative in the second part of the book covers the phases Healing, and Recovery.

Creative Acts of Healing complies with my Calendar of Mourning, Grief, Healing and Recovery.

MOURNING: The first three months after the birth stand by themselves, are disconnected from the newborn in the sense that a year before, the baby was merely -a being- in search of a human vessel; in the mind of its parents a wish, a mere idea, a longing, perhaps an aching in the belly.

For the parent these are the months of mourning over lost expectations; over not knowing, never having a chance to get to know, that new human being, their child.

GRIEF: After three months the initial period of mourning slides into that of grief. While body and mind get used to not having a baby to feed and care for, a woman's hormones still run rampant. She cannot recognize herself in this forlorn person.

During the following nine months the parents, especially the mother, are reminded of the pregnancy leading to the delivery and loss. They have to learn to live without the expectation, a challenge when memories of expecting are so clear and inevitable; there is always the last year this time.

Then there is the loss of interest in anything, followed by the urge to recover one's creativity. Recreation of what is lost proves to be impossible, what remains is the option to create something new. A reminder perhaps, a statement, an exclamation mark, the scream made visible on paper.

HEALING: The following twelve months start with the anniversary of the birth and the loss; while a benevolent veil softens the edges, recollection of the loss may hit at unexpected moments.

Each and every month thereafter is an anniversary of mourning or grief combined with recovery. In time, memories of pain are layered with new experiences.

Through reading, communication with other bereaved parents and by creative acts, the parents are able to give a place in their lives to the child they lost.

RECOVERY: After the loss, every added year brings new grief, over the child one never sees growing up. Seeing a little girl or boy of the age the lost child could have been, brings sadness. Grieving is a never-ending process. But along the way trust in one's self and in care givers will be restored. Mourning is tearing clothes, sheets and fabrics related to the lost loved one. Grief is holding on to the shreds and arranging them. Healing lies in patching the pieces together. Recovery is found stitch by stitch. No one is lost forever.

Judith van Praag
Seattle, December, 1998

LOSS

Monday, January 11 1993.

Four-fifty-five A.M. I am sitting on a vinyl covered chair in the recreation room of the hospital, staring past my reflection in the window. What happened? Why am I acting so cool? Has sadness got stuck in my head? Outside, the dark sky sheds heavy drops on the asphalt of the bike-path, forming dark puddles of rain water, red like blood, colored by the halted trams' reflector lights.

I feel numb, there is this dullness of the senses, except for the ache in my perineum and vulva, there where I sit on the stitches. Stitches, for I was torn, cut and sewn. Mike, my love and lover, husband and father of my child, sleeps in the twin bed of our hospital room. From where I sit, in the television lounge, I can see the sign on our door "silence please, couple sleeps." They say it is good to sit on your stitches, even when it hurts. The fluid will drain out of the wound and that helps the healing process. When I am in bed I am supposed to wear a mini-pad that's been wetted and frozen into a solid white chunk of ice, inside the diaper sized sanitary napkin. That is to bring down the swellings and bruises around my vagina and anus. I have delivered. We delivered a beautiful baby-girl.

Her name is ARIANE EIRA. She is dead. Our baby is dead. Our daughter never saw the light. Her feet, legs, torso, arms and shoulders were born into the cold of this world, while her sweet face stayed inside of me. She suffocated. The doctors tell us they think she got stuck with her chin behind my pelvic bone. Was it my inadequacy? Had I not pushed hard enough? Both doctors assured me that I did well, throughout the delivery, labor without epidural.

I feel removed from reality in an odd way. Is that nature's way of helping me cope? To make me feel so numb. The impersonal decorations of this room; some thrown together office furniture, an old television set, dog-eared magazines on a metal table, the flickering neon light, the darkness outside, it makes me feel like I have been removed from my own world. A warmer, kinder, colorful world. What happened, what was the sequence of events?

1998

When I look at my journal of January 1993, I see pages and pages of repetition. I describe how my water broke on Friday morning, how my husband Mike nearly collapsed in the bathroom, shaky with nervous anticipation. I wrote about the trip to the hospital, the kind cabby and about the intake at the maternity ward. I penned sentence after sentence about waiting for the contractions to start. I wrote about bonding with nurse Margie during the worst pains and how I dove into the tidal waves of her irises, spiraled into the deep blue sea of her eyes, until I'd hit the sudden quiet center of the storm, inside the darkness of the pupil. I wrote about digging my fingernails in the flesh of Mike and my coach Kay's hands, I wrote about waiting for the doctor to come, waiting for the head of my breech baby to come out while her body had already been born.., waiting for the medical team to tell us our baby had died.

Five years ago, I wrote about everything, except the pain of loss. I did not have words for my loss, I did not know the language of grief.

All through my childhood and while growing up, whenever I had a little accident, I heard my mother use the phrase: "Brand is erger," or: Fire is worse. If I'd break a glass she'd say "Scherven brengen geluk," or: Chards bring good luck.

My mother's love for the grandmother I never knew (she died before I was born), was reflected in language. Mama would toss what I later learned were cliches at me, followed by the referent words: "My dear mother always spoke in proverbs and sayings."

For my grandmother, born in 1871, proverbial sayings were not the platitudes we regard them as today. Words we now encounter in folksy display, written in fluid paint on decorated saws, reflect the practical view of life of the days of old. Sayings we now know as cliches, once were the wisdom our ancestors lived by.

Hearing my mother use words passed on from her mother, taught me my mother tongue and helped me in my understanding of language. Her reaction whenever I dropped something was almost philosophical, yet she never taught me the language of grief.

"Fire is worse," she'd say when I'd tear my pants in play,or spilled cocoa on the table cloth; those words were miracle healers when I was a child. But it wasn't until recently when I found myself humming a half forgotten nursery rhyme, that I was able to add the latter part, which gave totally new meaning to my mother's words. Sung in canon it goes like this:

> Brand is erger, brand is erger.
> Brand brand! Brand, brand!
> En daar is geen water...
> en daar is geen water.

There is a fire but no hope for recovery, for there is no water to douse the flames. Only the first line had stuck in my mother's mind, fire was worse than anything that could happen. That is, until I lost my baby. And then, she had no words but the wrong ones.

For as long as I can remember, feeling emotions equaled the discomfort of indigestion, an unpleasant feeling I learned to distinguish from constipation thanks to years of therapy and self reflection. With the help of many compassionate friends I have learned the language of grief.

As every living language the language of grief starts by shaping the lips, by opening the mouth, by uttering a sound. The language of grief starts by saying the first letter of the name of the lost one out loud.

Start with the first letter of the name. Whisper it, hiss it, grumble it. Add a vowel if the first letter is a consonant. Give air to the letters. Breathe in, and on the -out- let a sound come out of your throat. If it's a sound of agony, let it come out. Do this, over and over again until you've done so enough (you'll know).

Spell the letters of the whole name and say out loud: This is the name of my loved one. This is the name I will not forget. This is the name I will use to remember her(him) by. This is the name I will say out loud. The memory lives on in the name I will not forget.

The language of grief starts by saying the name of the lost loved one out loud.

&

MOURNING

Thursday January 14, 1993

Home again on Wittenburg, in our strangely cheerful apartment overlooking the canal. Neither the salmon, vanilla, and pistachio colored walls, nor the violet floors speak of the tragedy in our lives. Our plants are still green, the sparrows still land on the balcony.

Kay picked us up at the hospital. She found a parking place in our street block, but not quite in front of the entrance of our apartment building. Embarrassed to come home without my baby, I glanced at the neighboring flats. There was nobody to witness my shame. Kay went upstairs with us. She did not stay long.

"You've got to go through it, be on your own again," she said giving us both a big hug. "I'll call you to hear how you're doing."

Fifteen minutes after she left, a buzz told us somebody was downstairs at the front door.

"I can't talk to anybody," I said. Mike nodded and walked over to the hallway to answer the intercom. I heard him unlock the apartment door.

"I'm sorry Judith, it's your friend Tina, she says she just wants to drop something off."

"Okay, Tina is cool." With the door ajar I could hear the resonance of her running feet on the stairs. She pushed open the door and entered panting. Her face and eyes, red from crying, were nearly hidden behind an enormous bunch of long stemmed yellow roses. Nodding at Mike she handed him the flowers and rushed over to me.

"Oh, I feel so bad for you," she dropped a pair of black high tops on the couch beside me. "You need some sturdy shoes to support you girl!" She hugged me hard, then turned to Mike, "I'm sorry, I did not mean to ignore you, I am so sorry for both of you." She hugged him as well, while Mike held the flowers away from their embrace. "Let me take care of those, I know my way around, and then I'll be out of here," Tina volunteered. She found an enameled bucket for the roses, took care of the arrangement and left as rapidly as she had entered after kissing me once more.

"I would never have thought of using that bucket," Mike said stunned by the whirlwind visit.

"Yes, Tina is amazing," I agreed, "She's got a way with things."

Friday January 15

Joanita, my counselor, convinced me to ask Family Services for help around the house. "If you had brought your baby home you would have got help. Even without ARIANE here, you are still a mother recovering from a delivery."

I seem to be in some sort of stupor, I feel neither hot nor cold. Now and then tears roll down my cheeks. I know that what has happened is terrible, yet I seem to be without feeling. I cannot even think about the ceremony last Wednesday. I want to write about it for our friends and family abroad, but I cannot think about that day. Joanita said I am in a state of shock.

1998

You're in shock when you can't believe what happened to you, when every cell in your body screams: No it isn't true.

Until I held ARIANE EIRA in my arms, I couldn't really believe I was going to have a baby, silly as that may sound. And then she was there, perfect. Yet, her eyes closed, her body limp, her skin pale except for burgundy lips.

I do not know how we would have survived without the help from kind strangers or tokens of love and compassion from our friends. Tina was the first of many who visited us at our home to mourn the loss of our baby.

"Don't hesitate to ask for favors," Kay stressed while we were still at the hospital, "Your friends will be more than happy to oblige, go ahead call Josephine and ask her to take care of your first dinner at home."

So I did. And after Tina left, Josephine came and unpacked a pile of plastic dishes filled with Indonesian delicacies she had cooked for us. We hardly spoke. After she dished out the food she sat for a while, her hands together, quietly, then she left. Where our friend had been silent, the food spoke for her; the stewed poultry's skin golden-brown with ketjap, the flavor warm with spices and herbs, the white rice cooked just right, the green beans kissed by garlic and red pepper.

The help sent by Family Services was in her sixties. After my shower on the first morning at home, she helped me put a make-shift brassiere on. Pulling the two folded diapers tightly around my torso (meant to keep the milk flow down), she sighed. I thought with exertion. During her coffee break she told me how she had lost her first born after five days.

"I had eight children after that, but I'll never forget that first one," she stirred her coffee hard, head bent.

In the beginning I felt embarrassed by my inability to be a good hostess and by all of our friends' attention. Propped up against pillows on our sofa-bed, I was baffled by their wish to hear what had happened. At first I was reluctant to tell our visitors, but once I got started I couldn't stop and I surprised myself by how often I could tell the story of ARIANE EIRA's delivery and death. Mike listened, nodding his head in agreement.

Jeannette surprised me with eau de toilette, Broes and Hagar presented me with tiny golden ear studs. Mementos for our little girl.

Broes offered to take some of the birth and passing announcement cards to distribute them at the neighborhood stores.

"The shopkeepers have watched you grow. Hagar and I can inform them of the outcome and that way we'll prevent uncomfortable encounters in the future."

What foresight! We wouldn't have thought of doing that. The following weeks I was even more grateful each and every time I passed the butcher store, the greengrocer or bakery. I sunk my head between my shoulders so that I wouldn't have to face anybody. I felt ashamed that I had come home without our baby.

Asking for help was not something the members of my family did easily. Asking for help meant you had to acknowledge you couldn't do something yourself. Asking for help showed your vulnerability. Even after losing my baby, asking for help was difficult, but once I experienced the loving care and understood how good it made the other(s) feel, asking for help became a little bit easier.

Thursday January 21, 1993

Said to Mike yesterday, and today again, how the -live- image of ARIANE is starting to fade. It is harder day by day, to focus on her face, to remember her the way she looked when we held her in our arms. Foggy layers are coming between her and me. Mike says I don't need to be afraid of forgetting her. I know he's right, but I'll have to revert to photographs. The Polaroids Margie made, and Kay's pictures, are all that remain of her image in the material world. We talked about the spiritual and the material understanding -if you can speak of understanding in this situation.

When I think of ARIANE as a spirit who will always stay with us, I can deal with the loss. However, in the material world, seeing the things we collected for her arrival; the carriage, the outfits I knitted; merely passing by the door of the empty baby room, makes her absence apparent. I miss her physical presence. Mike reminds me that my own physical state; the natural expectancy to nurse my baby, to care for her, and the hormonal imbalance, makes the reality of the loss come down extra hard.

We have received so many reactions. Even from people who only heard about our tragedy through others. By now there is a stack of cards and letters. I keep them with the remainder of the announcements in the box from the printer. The orange cardboard box has become a treasure chest. Beside the correspondence, it contains the envelope with photos of ARIANE. I keep it on the table next to my place on the couch. Every now and then, I reread something. Somehow I am not able to call anybody. When someone calls us, I am glad to talk, to tell what has happened.

Saturday January 23

"I like to think of ARIANE as the sun," Mike seated in the rocker, still in his bathrobe, soaked up bashful rays entering our room through one of the windowpanes.

I fold diapers. Not in a shape suitable for little baby buns, but only to bind off my titties. To make the milk flow stop. Ouch!

We've caught ourselves laughing at funny things on television. At first we were shocked, then we agreed we honor our precious daughter by going on with our lives. It happens, that we are watching a comedy show on the telly, when the phone rings. We look at each other—compose ourselves. At times the grief of the caller, on the other side of the line throws the reality of life without ARIANE in our faces. We wish to recuperate, to recover our strength and lust for life.

Sunday January 31

My cousin Zia came for a visit with her husband and child. While the men talked about America and the little girl worked on a drawing for Mike and me, Zia told me about her Caesarean, the breech delivery and -if only. My stomach and chest tightened. While talking about my sorrow, she related her experience and had already decided for herself that hers and mine are the same. I listened to her as she talked about her feelings of insecurity after the C-section. I have heard that before, how women who do not get a chance to go through natural childbirth, feel as though they have been cheated out of something. I didn't want to listen any longer, I cut her off.

"No, I don't feel insecure, I feel plain hurt, to have memories of myself being pregnant, to remember the delivery and now not having ARIANE. I feel deprived of holding my baby ARIANE EIRA in my arms."

We have noticed how other people grab the opportunity to deal with their own pain when confronted with our loss. That is fine, but I cannot stand it when they start comparing their hurt with ours. And -what if- doesn't help me at all.

When we are out walking, I look into prams, curious to see the little faces. Strollers don't attract me that much. It's perambulators with lacy sheets and warm covers in which little princes and princesses are hidden from view, that make me want to stop and peek in. Mike, trying to protect me from myself, urges me to walk on. But I want to see the little faces. Perhaps he is trying to protect himself.

During the night, I wake up, thinking of ARIANE. Never fantasies or pleasant thoughts. Usually memories of the delivery. They repeat themselves, until I'm in a waking nightmare and I get up. I stay up for a while and then return to bed. When I wake up in the morning the memory of the dream returns, but at least I'm really awake and the day has started.

Earlier today Mike went out to get money from the ATM next to the Artis Zoo entrance. The machine was shut down, and he came back feeling frustrated. Instead of making an attempt to find another machine in our area, for instance the one near the Waterloo Flea market, he came straight home. The sight of women with babies and children at the Zoo had made him sad. He wonders about the fluctuation of his feelings, as I do about mine. At times I wonder why I am feeling so depressed, to be brought back to our reality: life without our daughter. The pain continues.

Amsterdam, January 1993
Letter to friends and family.

ARIANA/ARIANE: Welsh "Like Silver" (from ARIADNE Greek the Mythological daughter of Cretan King MINOS, who gave THESEUS a thread to guide him out of the maze-like prison known as the labyrinth. EIRA: Welsh "Like Snow" a pretty name for a winter baby.

Dearest,
"A baby with a mind of her own," the gynecologist said. ARIANE EIRA was in breech position. However, a C-section may involve risks for both mother and child, and as the odds for natural childbirth were good, the team of gynecologists decided for the latter. After carefully monitoring us, for hours after the water had broken at 5:00 A.M., labor was induced by an infusion of medication at 1:20 P.M.

Mike and our friend Kay were wonderful coaches all through labor and delivery and doctors and nurses did what was within their power. All went well until the very end -the breech nightmare. We lost our beautiful little girl the moment we received her.

ARIANE EIRA was born and passed on: Friday the 8th of January at 8:00 P.M. Resuscitation failed. The whole deliverance team plus the pediatrician stood at my bed-side, looking grave, as the gynecologist broke the news -our daughter was dead. The nurse brought her to us, our SNOW-WHITE, wrapped in a receiving blanket. We held her in our arms and admired her perfect features; Mike's lips, like dark rose petals against the ivory white of the smooth skin, his small ears; my curly hair, in tiny blond springs on her head, and whose nose might she have? We tried to take it all in, the length of her legs, the long toes and fingers, all twenty of her nails... We kissed her. But it did not bring her back. We told her about our dreams and that we loved her and that we always will...

We spent a week in the hospital, where the quiet combined with the attention from the staff and our loving friends made an intensive grieving possible.

On Wednesday the 13th at 9:30 A.M. the service for ARIANE EIRA was held at the crematorium Westgaarde on the outskirts of Amsterdam.

The small coffin was draped with a white satin cover, on it friends and family placed bouquets with tiny flowers; a single rose from my cousin's six-year-old. The pianist played lullabies on the grand piano; first one by SCHUBERT, and when the floor receded and the coffin went down, one by BRAHMS. The music was beautiful and we could imagine ARIANE EIRA dancing away on it, surrounded by flowers into the close distance of the eternal fields. MOZART's lullaby sounded from the piano as we left the auditorium. The others followed us into the family room; it was time for hugs and words of comfort. We were relieved to find the ritual a soothing experience and it made it easier for the others to share their feelings with us.

There is no blame, no guilt, WHY? is all there is left. There are no words for it and still there is the urge to share our grief with family and friends. When we do so, feeling compassion and support helps us to recover, which in turn helps the other one(s) in facing us.

1998

This letter reads like a half truth or half lie. Nothing about the unkept promise of a C-section if I had not dilated sufficiently by 6:00 P.M. Nothing about the doctor who made me wait until she had finished her dinner, nor about the brutal delivery, or the agonizing images carved in our minds of our baby stuck with her head inside of me.

In 1993 I needed to write about my living nightmare in the most positive way or I feared I would blow up in anger. I was afraid I'd become embittered, disappointed in people forever, enraged with the unfairness of it all. I couldn't afford to get angry, I thought. Perhaps I would go crazy and would never have recovered. I did not want to be Judith, who lost her baby and went insane. Our American friends wondered why we would not sue the doctor, the hospital. They were angry for us it seemed.

Is the answer to the questions: How do you survive the loss of your baby? What do you do with your anger? answered by prosecuting the doctor involved?

Unleashing anger after loss is a healthful action for bereaved parents. Letting the world know how devastated they are, is part of mourning and grief. A process that may take years and should not be looked upon lightly when the lost one is -merely- a baby.

Good doctors sometimes make bad decisions and they need to be reprimanded. At the same time we all need to be reminded that notwithstanding the awe-inspiring developments in this age of technology, the realm of life and death is still an area we don't have unrestricted power or total control over.

Instead of suggesting a lawsuit to parents bereft of their newborn, the bereft and society ought to be advised about the process of mourning and grief. Infant death is a serious loss, a loss parents may not automatically get over: with the arrival of another baby and when they have so much else to live for.

Immediately following the death of their baby, parents are in a state of shock and most vulnerable to any kind of input. If suing is presented as a way to get even, they will eagerly take that chance. Bereaved parents will do anything to quiet the tormenting voices of guilt, fear and pain that demand an answer to the unanswerable: WHY?

Bereaved parents are not helped by callous lawyers. What they need is a support group of compassionate friends and family, a community that helps them through the times of hardship that have befallen them. They need to be made aware of the nature of mourning and grief, of hope and life after hope.

Writing about loss is good therapy. You can start small, in the margin of the newspaper, on the back of a paper napkin, on a 3x5 card. You can buy a note-book for a buck, a fancy journal, or use your calendar. Write at the spur of the moment, on the doily of a pastry you just ate, on a brown paper bag, on a coaster. Start with a doodle, start with the name of your lost love, or just words that come up in your mind. Write the syllables stuck in your throat, write the words weighing on your shoulders, write the same thing over and over. Write a letter to a friend, a relative, or someone long gone. As you write you create a gauge by which weeks, months, years later your recovery may be measured.

Thursday February 4, 1993

Mike has not played his guitar since the evening two days before Christmas when I was hyperventilating after we found out that our baby was in breech.

I'm bothered by a troublesome thought. Could anybody have stood up for me during my labor? I had been promised a C-section if I had not dilated enough by 6:00 P.M. When I said I did not want to go on, it was not out of lack of gusto, I truly feared our child would suffocate. The intern did not have the power to convince the ob/gyn who was still at home. My sweet Mike, the poor guy, an American in Amsterdam, literally did not understand what was going on. Everybody around us spoke in Dutch.

1998

For years I have consulted the *I Ching*, the ancient Chinese oracle. Whenever I felt unsure about a situation or a relationship I'd throw my three coins to find solace in the wise words. Before we left for the Netherlands, Mike's mother gave us a *Book of Runes* that came with a velvet bag filled with stone pieces engraved with symbols. You meditate on a question in your mind, then you let your fingers do the searching in the bag. When a certain piece speaks to you, when it sticks to your fingers, you pull it out and lay it down. Then you look up the symbol in the index of the book and read what is said. More often than not I am stunned by the accuracy of the oracle. I will cast the Viking Runes. If anything the oracle will give me something to meditate on, something to help me deal with the negative thoughts.

In times of distress meditation works soothing, as does prayer, or going for a long walk in the woods or on the beach. The magical cycle of waves that roll, unfold, pull back, roll unfold, pull back, restores the trust in continuation.

Friday February 5, 1993

Am not holding my water. Find it distressful. Apart from the aspect of discomfort, it reminds me again of our loss. When I say -delivery- or -childbirth-, I *see* ARIANE coming out of me. Each time is like a scream, over and over again. When someone calls to ask how I'm doing, what am I to say? That I'm doing well? Oh, Lordy, Lordy.

Mike and I kiss and love each other the way we can right now. We're both looking forward to the day that we'll be able to make love completely again.

The morning that we were to go home from the hospital, a day after the cremation, the intern entered the room and positioned himself at the foot of the bed.

"Not that I think you'd want to do anything right now," he smiled apologetically, "But remember that the medication you got to stop the milk flow, makes you fertile immediately. I suggest you think about a contraceptive to use."

Saturday February 6

Nightmares while awake. Every space in my mind occupied by memories not of ARIANE in my arms, but by recollections of pregnancy or delivery. I see myself big, happily posing for photographs in the nude, in leotards, in street clothes. I remember sleeping with six pillows, how I could barely walk the last week, how we ate lamb kebab the evening before my water broke. Then the high waves of labor, the power that tormented my body, and most painful of all, the brutal images of a bloody baby who can not come out of me. No memories of a live baby, of our child growing up. I always knew there could be nothing worse than losing a child. I had a hard time understanding a friend in Los Angeles, who had lost her fifteen year old daughter, when she said: "...it is great to have had a daughter." Now I think I understand better. The thought of not having any memories apart from those of delivery and of holding the little dead person in my arms is devastating. Any thought may evoke the memories. When I think of somebody for instance, I may have seen that person during the pregnancy. Then the next thought is: How to explain? And again images of the delivery surface, raw and crude.

1998

Meanwhile I have learned from Penny Simkin, a licensed physical therapist, childbirth educator and the president of the Doulas of North America, that a woman who has gone through a traumatic delivery often will suffer from Post Traumatic Stress Disorder, somewhat the same way as a Vietnam veteran. As quoted from an interview in Synapse: "She'll have nightmares, hallucinations, flashbacks, preoccupation and crying spells.

Symptoms which should not be confused with those of post-partum depression."

Sunday February 7, 1993

Our downstairs neighbor misunderstood the English text announcing ARIANE'S birth and passing. She sent a shocking pink card with a happy little shepherd girl on a swing saying, "Congratulations with your daughter." I wrote the woman a note, to make sure that the poor soul won't feel bad when she finds out our baby will never come home.

A bright turquoise card came to our surprise from Jason, a friend whose mother tongue is English. I sent him a letter explaining we lost ARIANE. Today we talked on the phone.

"How could I of all people..," he stammered.

"You just wished us well, I guess you did not wish to read the bad news."

I complained to him that I'm old and still don't have a child. He jumped on that.

"You are wrong. ARIANE has given you time. She was with you for nine months, you had a full term pregnancy. And you went through the delivery. You are not a thirty-seven-year-old childless woman who feels the biological clock ticking, you already had a baby! Having gone through all that has made your body stronger."

Feeling the way I did I could barely agree with that last line, but I understood his point.

My writer friend Bella called from Los Angeles. I told her that ARIANE had been cremated, and that her ashes have been dispersed at sea so that her spirit will be everywhere, and not tied to a place by a grave. Bella added that ARIANE's spirit is in the ocean and in the flowers.

Monday February 8

Our ARIANE EIRA one month.

Tuesday February 9

Mike and I never had our "Beschuit met Muisjes." The anise in the "muisjes" stimulates milk flow, something I did not need of course. I had my rusk this morning. Six of them (!) while Mike was in the shower.

After that I started a load of laundry which had been sitting in the machine, and went into the baby room, once again merely the small room. I took the baby bath, filled it with bottles and nipples and warm water bottles and all the little things we won't be needing now. I set it on the baby carriage, topping it off with the dressing pillow.

1998

We don't do baby showers in The Netherlands. Before ARIANE was born I felt sorry about that, after her birth I felt relieved that we were not left with a pile of gifts. The Dutch have far too much common sense to celebrate before a baby is born. Wait and see, is the motto. Visitors come for a "kraambezoek," after your baby is born. They come by appointment, to prevent that the "kraamvrouw," the mother of the newborn child, will be worn out by too many admirers at the same time. Tradition wants that each guest gets a special treat during this visit. "Beschuit met muisjes." "Beschuit," Dutch rusk, is a common breakfast food, eaten with sweet or savory toppings. "Muisjes," are anise seeds, with a pink and white sugar coating (lately there is also blue and white for boys), from which the sprig of the seed, or mouse tail sticks.

"We don't do showers in Holland," is what I say when I am invited to a shower, but cannot bear to go. "We do 'beschuit met muisjes,' and we'll be happy to come after your baby is born."

Our friends seem pleased with that solution, for however much they would like to act -normal, what has happened to us is every parents' worst nightmare and our presence is only a reminder of what can go wrong.

Sunday February 14 1993

It is a good thing that I made contact with Joanita, my social worker, before ARIANE was born; after Kay informed her what had happened she took care of all the paper-work, making sure we'd receive financial aid. On the 4th I had a counseling session with her on the phone.

Mike and I have to reacquaint ourselves with each other all over again, she said. We are parents, but not in practice. After months of anticipating parenthood, we are merely a couple, individuals who have to learn to appreciate each other as such. Since I got pregnant shortly after we met, we don't have much history together as just a couple. Still we can look back on our camaraderie, our working together, our love, the sharing of our tragedy.

Thursday February 18

And now, it is no longer the nightmare that repeats itself, seeing ARIANE's half-way birth. Instead I feel the -hole- the lack. I find myself thinking about ARIANE, the growing child. I miss pushing her pram, bathing, dressing, feeding her. It is as though I'm trying to find her -in my mind searching my memories for her hiding place, for an image portraying my little girl.

It is as though this was meant to be, forgetting and remembering. Whenever I remember acutely, I feel bad for the times that I momentarily forgot about our loss. The hours that pass are filled with regular activities; chores around the house, a movie in the Tuschinsky Theater, the first evening visit with friends. Then, I suddenly remember, or rather, I search for memories, which I cannot find. Like a cat who's looking for her kittens. I'm looking for ARIANE and I cannot find her.

Friday February 19

On the way to my hairdresser, I ran into Ellen, a fellow designer. We spotted each other when we were still way apart. I got tears in my eyes and when we were close enough, I saw tears running down her cheeks. We stood face to face crying. There was no need to talk. We hugged before we resumed our separate ways.

ڽ ڽ ڽ

To Ellen and Every Other
Through me you move
as I move through you
our tears mingle
when our paths cross
you am I am you
when our paths cross
our tears mingle
as you move through me
through you I move

ڽ ڽ ڽ

Wednesday February 24
As time goes by and life goes on.

Second night in a row that I did not sleep well. I clearly remember looking at the alarm clock at exactly 3.33 A.M.

Mike and I have made love again, all the way. I still don't feel we can do just anything; I am still touchy where the stitches are concerned, but other than that, all is fine.

The other day I had to fill out a form which hopefully will lead to financial aid in paying for the cremation bill and the bill from the printer. One of the questions was: What was your relationship to the deceased. I wrote: Mother. It did something special to me. Mother, I am somebody's mother. Even though the somebody in question has gone.

I'm itching to work on my art again. The above poem is the first I have written in a long time. I've got to get started. Create, because it will help me. It will help me digest what has happened and it will help me find perspective again. Create around our loss.

ॐॐॐ

SPOONING

My love in fetal position/
takes the place of the empty feeling/
the vacated belly/
our baby's home for nine months/
once again we're like newlyweds/
our by winter-gear hooded kisses
protected from the gazes of passers-by/
we're parents without responsibilities/
except for ourselves/each-other/
the memory of our child/
no cradle to rock/no pram to push/
no feeding during the night/
we sleep next to the vacant room/
where winter's cold/ combined with grief/
drives us closer/ than love in a warm climate would do/
back to point zero/where we started/
but for the history we now share/
making us one/once again

ॐॐॐ

Thursday February 25

Mike and I went to the hospital for the follow-up talk with the obstetrician/gynecologist. We bravely watched pregnant women passing through the waiting room of her office.

Mike squeezed my hand. The doctor who promised me a C-section, but who wasn't on call during the delivery, walked by with his assistant. Neither of them recognized us.

The obstetrician went over the results of the autopsy, the intern who had tried in vain to get me to the operating room, was present as well.

"Sad but true," the doctor sighed, "There was nothing wrong with ARIANE except for the lack of Oxygen. Not being a heavy baby may have contributed to the fact that the traumatic birth proved to be too much for her," she spoke as though reading the words from the pathologist's report. She was relieved to tell us she had not broken our baby's neck. I could have wrung hers on the spot.

Behind a screen in the same room, I let her perform a pelvic exam on me. How odd that was. As though nothing had happened. As if we did not share a horrible history. All is well down there though. If we want to we could try to get pregnant again any time we're ready for it.

"We owe you one," the doctor smiled opening the door for us.

We smiled back and shook hands. "Looking forward to seeing you back pregnant," she said. The intern nodded, he had not said one word after his initial greeting.

In the hallway women in all stages of expectancy were waiting for their appointments, some had small children with them. I wondered whether it would make a difference if you build up a relationship with an ob/gyn before going in for the delivery. Would they make sure you'd get what you were promised?

1998

When I got pregnant with ARIANE EIRA, I chose to be taken care of by midwives. In The Netherlands this was and is not an unusual choice.

"Midwives when you can, obstetrician/gynecologists when you have to," is a popular motto. Home birthing is encouraged and health insurance companies even give money after the delivery to women who do not make use of hospital facilities. The midwives of the birthing center I went to do not hide their aversion towards the birthing procedures common in hospitals and in their mind painkillers are a no-no. Women can be empowered by natural childbirth and the midwives help women under their care claim that power.

I was astonished when I heard that a girlfriend in America had received a sonar scan when she was only seven weeks pregnant. There was no medical indication, the scan was made merely for the fun of the parents, to see the little -bean- that would grow to be their baby.

"We only have sonar scans made when we are unsure about the situation the baby is in, or when there are problems during the pregnancy," one of the midwives of the birth center said.

When I was 37.5 weeks pregnant the junior midwife who examined me, suspected that what she had held for the head, nicely positioned, was really our baby's behind. She called in a senior colleague who confirmed the other's suspicion and immediately sent us to the obstetrician/gynecologist across the street whose office was affiliated with the midwives' center.

"Breech." This woman concluded. "You may go back to the midwives' office, they'll talk to you." The tone of her voice made her words sound like a verdict.

In retrospective, I know we should have been referred to the hospital at that point. That way we would have been able to build a relationship with the doctors there. I suggested as much but the midwives were adamant, they would take care of me. They even refused to give me information about a C-section.

"No need to worry about something that is not necessary yet."

We made an appointment for six o'clock the next day.

"Take a warm bath to relax beforehand and we'll try to turn your baby."

That evening I hyperventilated, lack of information made me scared. I called the midwives' help line.

"I understand you're afraid of the turning. If you're still scared tomorrow, you don't have to go along with it," the woman on the phone told me. "Breathe in a bag, put on warm pajamas, get in bed and listen to some nice music. I'm sure you'll feel better soon."

I did as I was told and Mike played the guitar until I was relaxed enough to doze off.

Since we did not have a tub at home, only a shower, I took a bath at my girlfriend Marjan's house, who lives close to the birth center. She went with me to the appointment. She had asked beforehand whether that would be all right with Mike, who thought it was a great idea. The manipulation was done without sonar scan and the midwives did not succeed.

"Now you've got to go to Rita with the golden hands. If she can't do it, nobody can," one said.

"Yes, and if she can't then we will give it another try," the other added.

When I told my friend Jeannette, who is a doctor herself, about the experience, she insisted I would call my general practitioner and get an immediate referral to the hospital.

"What a scandal. You're thirty-seven and with your first child!"

My general practitioner reacted the same way when I called her the next morning and she set up an appointment with an obstetrician at the hospital right away.

Two male doctors tried to turn our baby, while they kept a close look at the images produced by sonar scan. They did not have success either.

"If the baby stays in breech, you'll have a medical indication to deliver in the hospital."

"What about my midwife?"

"She will do the delivery and we will be on stand-by in case there are complications. Meanwhile you just go to your regular check-ups at the birth center. But I'd like to see you two days before your due date."

My midwife was furious when we showed up at the appointment time that afternoon.

"You went to the hospital on your own account."

"None of you would refer me."

"We could have."

"You wanted me to go see Rita and then try again yourselves."

"We wanted to give the midwives a chance."

WRONG. Wrong answer. Midwives, doctors, nurses, they all have to work for THE MOTHER. Until that moment I trusted that was a given.

On the day of my appointment with the doctors in the hospital, two days before my due date, at 5:00 A.M. my water broke. A doctor whom I had not met before did the intake. He explained to us how labor and delivery of a breech baby has to go through certain phases on a strict time schedule, like a train arriving at certain stations at a particular time.

"If you have not dilated sufficiently by 6:00 P.M.. we will give you a C-section," he patted me on the leg, "We'll monitor your baby's heart beat and keep an eye on you all day."
Unfortunately this doctor went off duty shortly after.

Notwithstanding four hours of heavy labor due to the chemicals that were dripping into my veins, I had no more than one centimeter dilation by 6:00 P.M.. and I was glad to see the intern leave. To get the operation room ready, I thought. But it turned out he had only called the doctor on duty that night.

"I'm sorry," he said, "She says you've got to continue a while longer."

I had no power, no air, between contractions to explain that I was not *just* saying I couldn't continue. I could not remind anybody of the promise made earlier that I would have a C-section by 6:00 PM.

Between 6:00 and 7:00 I dilated to 10 cm. Then I still had to wait with pushing until the doctor arrived at 7:30. By 7:55 our baby's body was born, except for her head. Use of forceps did not help, the knee of the intern on my belly did not help. Only after the doctor gave me an episiotomy, it became clear that our baby girl was stuck with her chin behind my pelvic bone. She suffocated in the last five minutes of the delivery.

I am convinced that if we had been able to secure a relationship prior to the delivery, the doctor might have had more interest in coming to the hospital when that was requested by the intern. She might have been more interested in what her colleague in the morning had said to me. She might have informed herself better about my state of being.

Even when a woman prefers a home birth and a doula and midwife as coaches, even when all looks good during the pregnancy, getting to know the hospital and obstetricians is a good idea.

Tuesday March 9, 1993

A lady from the welfare office called to tell me that the cost of the cremation will be covered by them.

"What happened?" she asked. I imagined her in her drab cubicle, a pile of dossiers on her desk, ours open in front of her. A total stranger showing compassion helped carry a little bit of my pain today.

Monday March 15

I am slamming kitchen-cabinet doors, rattling pans, burning the toast, mumbling under my breath. At times I break down in tears.

On Saturday, Mike and I went to the country. We walked through the forest and had tea with apple pie at a small restaurant at the edge of the moor. I told Mike I want to get pregnant again, but he is not ready. Every time we use a rubber, I feel I'm refused a pregnancy.

Thursday March 18

My counselor Joanita explained the difference between the grief over ARIANE's death and the sadness combined with anger I am experiencing lately, as pain over loss or death and pain over not being able to see our child, our daughter grow up. Having my bad temper thus explained soothes me somewhat; for the seemingly senseless tantrums were most disconcerting to me. With and without sense at the same time. I seemed to have been so sensible the first months and now suddenly I'll be overcome with emotion. Triggered by whatever.

Friday March 19

Mike was out when Reinie came by for a coffee chat. It was the first time we visited. So far we had only talked at art functions or in the street. We've known each other for years, but it was Mike and me losing ARIANE that brought us together under my roof. She handed me a potted plant with delicate flowers, shaped like Chinese lanterns. They're nearly translucent white with mauve line drawings on the bud leaves. I have never seen them before. Reinie said they grow in the wild in Scandinavia. I almost expected the flowers to start ringing, small voices to sound from nowhere.

"What happened?" she asked after I poured each of us a cup of coffee. As before with others who had granted me permission by asking, I was happy to reply. Every time it happens I am flustered by the other's focused attention for my story.

1998

Sensibility as a euphemism for shock. Where would I have been, where would I be, without coffee klatsch, the informal gathering for conversation. In Dutch: 'koffie krans' the circle of women, meeting to talk or gossip. Coffee means much more than a single-short-to go, or a double-tall two-percent latte, coffee means company. Having a coffee with someone means exchanging news, talking, listening, being listened to. You invite someone who needs support to come have 'een bakje troost,' a cup filled with solace. Where would I be without the never ending stream of compassionate people? It is impossible to go through the grief process alone. People need other people to heal, to stay healthy, to rekindle the flame of interest in life when that flame is on the verge of dying after a traumatic experience.

Saturday March 20, 1993

We've seen many movies lately. A delivery scene in *City of Joy,* took us by surprise. I cried during and after the birth of the breech baby to the leper parents. What irony, a perfectly healthy baby born to such badly deformed people. The child's position was turned by doctor Patrick before birth, something my real life doctors weren't able to do to ARIANE.

1998

I know now that watching the birth of any baby is enough to make my eyes flood. I feel emotional when I walk by a play-ground, I feel emotional after a visit with friends whose children are the same age ARIANE would have been. I feel emotional when I see how many women around me are pregnant.I feel emotional about children in need and children who are ill. And I will always feel emotional when I think of delivering my baby girl.

Thursday March 25

I paid a visit to Jean, one of the women of the pregnancy gym group. Small flat in the old-west part of town. She right away led me into the master-bedroom. Crib and commode were crammed between the parents' bed and a window facing the street. Seeing Jean's baby girl in her crib brought tears to my eyes.

"That's how ARIANE could have been," went through my mind. Jean insisted on me holding her baby. Whether it was Jean's anticipation or mine, the little girl started howling the minute her mother put her in my arms.

"Please take her away, she's upset."

Jean wouldn't hear of it. "She has no reason to act this way." She ushered me into the living-room and offered me a seat on the couch. I did not know what to do with the struggling baby, whose body tensed up completely, trying to escape from my hold, like the piglet from Alice in Wonderland's arms. Finally Jean gave in. Her baby quieted down immediately. From then on she sat staring at me with wide open eyes.

"She doesn't like my face," I said.

"I'm sorry, I don't know what got into her," Jean said.

"It is only natural," I said.

Over coffee Jean related her story. Since both she and her husband were older she'd had all the preliminary tests done to find any possible birth defects. They had known the sex of their baby from early on, but they kept it a secret from everybody else. Jean had been closely monitored and there had been no problems during the pregnancy. After the delivery she had been in very much pain. It turned out that she had been bruised internally and a swelling the size of a fist had formed and remained in her belly. It was good to listen to the perils of another woman who had given birth. But at the same time I realized how little we had in common, besides being mothers. After two and a half hours I was tired and wired from all the caffeine and wanted to go home.

"I'll go out for a walk, but this little girl needs a clean diaper," Jean got up, "Would you like to change her?"

"No, thanks." I did follow her into the bedroom. There was nothing during the visit or the walk later that hit me as hard as seeing the little girl's bare bottom. The creases in her legs, the smooth lips of her vagina, the little butt hole (from which the feces came squirting non-stop after Jean had just wiped it clean with tissues drenched in oil). One whole day later the image of the baby's bottom was still on my mind. It made me break down and weep. Those perfect pussy cheeks and lips...

ARIANE's sore little twit, the redness, the way it looked bruised. I shed some tears and Mike soothed me, surprised with my sadness over a little baby's vagina.

Friday March 26, 1993

While waiting for my coffee and roll at café Jaren, I read the Herald Tribune. At some point I met my own gaze in the wall high mirror twenty feet away from me. I was stunned by the notion I was the attractive woman I'd been staring at in the mirror. People paid attention to me, but I translated their glances in a negative way. Right then and there I became aware of how I have been feeling about myself. Negative.

Thought in the shower: I gave birth to my self when my baby died. I no longer am the child of my mother only. I am mother myself. Positive.

Tuesday March 30, 1993

My accountant called.

"You don't sound very enthusiastic," he said.

"Why should I."

"Well, with husband and child..."

I was quiet for a moment.

"You must have misunderstood our card. We lost ARIANE. Our baby is dead. But I appreciate your positive wishes for us." He stammered an apology. Boy, did he feel embarrassed.

Mike has the flu and went to bed after dinner. I had coffee and dessert with Marie, an old friend. She handed me a small box covered in blue marbled paper with gold trimming along the edges. I thought that was it.

"Open it," she said. Embedded in cotton lay the prettiest glass bottle I've ever laid my hands on. Delicate lilac with slight bulges, painted gold. It has a stopper and is meant to hold perfume or oil. Marie shrugged when I thanked her.

"Tell me what happened," she sat down on the sofa-bed.
I related the whole story. From the breaking of the water, through the delivery and the end. Marie cried. We cried. Then we talked about hemorrhoids. I didn't recall her mentioning painful swelling after the delivery of each of her two daughters, now two and four.

"You never told me," I said.

She grimaced, "Some things you only share with other mothers..."

1998

Ah, other mothers. I thank the other mothers who were willing to share their ailments and recovery with me. How I enjoyed talking about episiotomies, loss of abdominal muscles, hanging bellies, being able to make love again. After I lost my baby, most new mothers were reluctant to complain about anything. After all, they were holding their babies in their arms, what should they complain about? But I had given birth, I was sitting on the stitches, I had aching breasts and sore muscles as well. Other mothers got to talk about that at 'Mommy and Me.' I was alone with my husband, who, however supportive, could not really relate to the female issues. The focus had been so much on our loss, that it took me months before I dared ask Kay what the delivery had been like.

"Was mine a heavy delivery?" I asked.

"I would think so, you lost your baby."

"I mean, women talk about easy, or hard labor, what kind of labor did I have apart from the outcome?"

"Hard," she said.

But which woman dares to say to me that she had a hard labor while holding her babe in arms? Thank you again, to the mothers who were willing to talk the talk with me.

❧

LOST

In mourning I tear up
ten years of correspondence
and attempt to re-cycle
with the need to re-create.

The result a disappointing
grey-ish matter, not the
silky rough or rough silken
paper which breaths
on its own account:
handle with care.

A chlorine smell lingers on
as inerasable words drift
without direction or reason,
breakers intervening
with poetic flow

With this lack of function
I'm only facing
shredded paper illusions
incapable of competition
with the sharpest pain
the nearly unmentionable

LOSS

Lost

GRIEF

Thursday April 8
ARIANE 3 months.

What is it I want from Mike? I want the man back I fell in love with. I want him to do something that makes him happy. I want him to work on his career. Love alone is not enough. A week ago I cried out loud, that my love for him was not enough to make him believe in us, our future, our life together. And it is not. He needs to believe in himself. I have been minding his business too much, mothering him. Yesterday I realized that giving him the guitar stand for his birthday in March had been another wrong move, giving him the stand so that the naked guitar could beckon to be played on. So acting on impulse, I dissembled the stand. My gesture was taken the wrong way, he not only packed his instrument, but dragged the case over to the bedroom where he pushed it behind the clothes in his wardrobe. Another clash.

"Now you're really a guest, with only a wardrobe, nothing else to prove you live here," I said.

In the evening we went to a fringe theater show. A bad one. We left during the intermission, but going out was good for us.

We discussed the performance of the actors and the plot and I saw a glimpse of the man I used to know.

This morning I meditated while still in bed. Brought forward images I like: roses, tons of roses. And the beach, the sand under my feet. The breaking of sea-shells, the feeling of wet sand pressed between my toes. The sensation of having my feet licked by the ocean. Setting aside negative thoughts was not easy, but I managed.

1998

The midwife who came to see us at the hospital warned us that there would be a point from where we would start doing our own things again. That combined with the fact that every person has his or her own grief pattern might give us the idea that we were drifting apart. While we were so close, perhaps because of that, I did not realize at the time that Mike and I were already following our own path. I was angry with him, for not being what I wanted him to be, but in retrospect I can see how I was projecting my anger about our loss on our relationship and on him. He was sad and I wanted him to be happy, because I thought that would make me happy again.

Wednesday April 14, 1993

I have to specify my motivation for wanting to attend poet Derek Walcott's master classes.

Strange, I feel far removed from my past. What I did before ARIANE's birth doesn't seem to matter any more. Until now at least, for this other, nearly forgotten me is slowly stepping out of the fog.

Thursday April 15

Blew up in Mike's face in the morning, when he asked me how to get to the hairdresser's. I knew I was being unreasonable and apologized. I went to the gym, had a good work-out and then went to meet Mike at the salon. The girls think he is quite a hunk. They speak hardly any English, still he gets the picture. They're flirting with him in the mirrors and in a complimenting way smile hard at me.

We were supposed to meet Joanita in her office on the south side of the Vondel Park, so we bought sandwiches at the bakery and ate them in the park, on a bench across from the meadow shared by black and white cows, some goats, sheep, a llama, hens and a rooster. Mama brought me to the same park many a time. Seeing mothers behind strollers, or reaching out to stumbling toddlers learning to take their first steps made me glance at Mike, only to find him looking at me from the corner of his eyes.

Joanita suggested Mike and I would come to a session together after I told her how much we are in each other's hair. She listened to us and then cut straight through the crap.

"You may be trying to cut out and forget the possibly worst period in your life. To look back with regret at a successful single life and to want to retrieve that, is not strange at all."

Mike's presence becomes a major source of irritation because: I wish to be alone, or in other words single; I wish to erase the painful year.

She said that I need support and have to ask for it. Mike and I have a shared responsibility for our relationship. The assignment is to not *act* hatefully, but to just feel. We need to stay with our own feelings.

Monday April 19

In total darkness, the rooster in the backyard of the cafe across the canal, announces the break of day. Low above the houses a slice of moon. Birds are singing.

Thursday April 22

Around dinner time we went to Broes' thirty-first birthday party. The women in the family had prepared delicious food. All of Broes' favorite dishes; fish, fowl and lamb prepared in Mediterranean and Indonesian style.

About twenty-five guests, including seven children in party mode created a festive atmosphere. But I felt uncomfortable when Broes' sister and her best friend arrived, both heavily pregnant. They nodded at me, but walked immediately to the dining-room table where they sat down with their spouses. One of the men once made custom frames for my art-work, he barely acknowledged me. Like we are cursed or something. Perhaps they thought our bad luck might be contagious. I would have liked so much to sit with them and talk, about pregnancy and motherhood. Instead Mike and I sat together in easy chairs at the coffee table. Broes' great-grandmother, unaware of our predicament, started a conversation and we chatted amiably about her house in the stylish 'Betondorp' and her favorite hobby, painting. She urged us to come visit her some time. Broes' and Hagar's children were all over Mike, trying to make him speak Dutch and screaming with laughter whenever he made an attempt. After I finished eating, I took my plate to the kitchen, where Broes' mother was dishing out sherbet, ice-cream and fresh strawberries. Hagar's mother was distributing the luscious red fruit over thirty bowls and cups of odd design. Standing in the middle of a buzzing commotion, created by small and big children yelling out their preferences, I felt overcome with sadness and spooned my dessert into a creamy mush. Elsa, the wife of Broes' father was rinsing dishes and watched me pour the melted substance in the sink.

"I'm so sorry about your loss," she looked sideways at me handing me a tea-towel. I started drying the washed and rinsed off plates Elsa put in the strainer.

"What happened, would you mind telling me?"
Quietly I told her what had happened during the delivery. I felt great relief being able to acknowledge our loss. The sadness in my heart was diluted by the water running from the faucet, the tears dried up inside of me while I wiped the forks and knives, plates and glasses.

Elsa's husband clearly wished to say something as well. From the moment Mike and I arrived, I noticed him smiling at me from across the room in an awkward manner, but he never made his way over to talk. After Mike and I finished our coffee, we went home.

Friday April 30

Mike's first impression of Queen's day: "One big garage and yard-sale throughout the city."

We took our bikes and rode them around rather than through downtown, in order not to get caught in the crowds, and locked them to a lantern pole near the east side entrance to the Vondel park. Lawns and paths in the park had been reserved for the youngest vendors and performers. Suddenly we were eye to eye with a friend who sent flowers to the memorial service for ARIANE but whom we had not talked to yet. We just stood there, surrounded by jesters, screaming clowns and children singing praise of their merchandise. I shrugged and made a funny face. Our friend pulled up her shoulders and mimicked a clown.

"How are you doing?" she asked.

"Enjoying the day," I answered, looking at Mike who nodded. "Okay," she said. We hugged and went on our way.

Saturday May 1

We have been married for one year.

At times I wonder: Is this as bad as it can get? When will the pain, the insecurity, the anger cease? Or is this the beginning? Then I feel anxious about today, tomorrow, the future. You never know how much and what you'll get. What's next. Will I be healthy, will I be rich? Que sera, sera. What will be, will be.

Sunday May 2

Joanita's advice: Give yourselves a break. Take some vacation. Enjoy each other's company.

She clearly sees our relationship—no differences, only emotions. We need to figure out what our common goal is, but she doesn't think the time is right to start relationship therapy.

Monday May 3

When I started at the L.A. Women's Gym in 1989, I weighed 165 pounds. After a few months I had shed ten pounds. My weight was stable at 155 when I got pregnant. Now I weigh 183 pounds. So I am eighteen pounds heavier than at my most overweight time. ARIANE was light. My placenta was small. I gained where my baby should have. To be seen as fat only, hurts my feelings. If I'd be pushing a pram, people would look at me differently. Now I'm merely a big-bellied gal. I met Leo, the owner of my favorite Surinamese restaurant at the outdoors market.

"You've gotten big, yeah, well, Biiig!" He shook his head as though he didn't know what to make of it. Apparently he had missed seeing me pregnant and didn't know what had happened either. I did not feel like making him any wiser.

My California buddy Richard and his wife had a baby boy. When Rich's mother told me the infant keeps them awake at night, a wave of pain welled up in my chest. Always that sadness, to miss seeing ARIANE grow up. How blessed I'd feel if our baby was keeping us up at night. As it is, I merely wake up during the night with a restless feeling.

Mike and I went to the Contemporary Art Museum. Downstairs we enjoyed an exhibition of Ingo Maurer's work; lamps and whimsical lighting systems. His work is ingenious and at the same time poetic in its simplicity. As the son of a fisherman and self-proclaimed inventor he must have studied the ever changing effect of light upon water. As an adult he makes magic. Then upstairs, the permanent collection displayed in a totally new way against tinted walls; the idea of the new director.

Wednesday May 5

Liberation Day. Today, as on Queen's day again festivities and street sales, this time to celebrate the end of German occupation in 1945.

The 4th of May is Memorial Day in the Netherlands. To commemorate all those who were killed or slain during the Second World War, all of Holland practices two minutes of silence at 8:00 P.M. Traffic stops, radios and stereo systems are turned down, the proceedings at the World War Two monument in Amsterdam on the Dam square are broadcasted live on television, without commentary or music.

Last night Mike accompanied me to the "Hollandse Schouwburg," the Dutch, or in popular speech, Jewish Play house, for the 8:00 P.M. memorial service. It was from there that the Jews were rounded up to be taken to the concentration camps. The building has been restored, but the architectural state it was in after the war, has been respected.

As we approached, a steady stream of people like ourselves hurried toward the open doors. Behind the beautifully restored facade a surprise awaited us. On the right hand side is a glass enclosed exhibition area, where Jewish life before and after the war is represented by photographs.

On the other side, a similar space is reserved for a stunning account displayed on the wall. In green neon letters the family names of those who never returned drew our immediate attention.

As one of the speakers of the memorial service remarked: "It is a bittersweet idea to know that there finally is a place in Amsterdam where one can go to see the name of a relative or loved one. In seeing the names, among all the others, one is able to recreate the image and to respect the commemoration even more than before."

Saturday May 8
ARIANE four months.

I treated myself to a weekend paper making work-shop. Something new, something constructive. Four other novices and I watched mechanically shredded computer print-outs swish to a smooth pulp in a house-hold blender, before we each couched our own sheets. Smooth, clouded creations. We tore our teacher's discarded drawings on acid free paper, mixed the snippets with warm water and gelatin and stirred the murky paper soup in a three-gallon bucket, working hard to keep the drill with the mixing attachment from flying out of orbit. I enjoyed myself. Only on my way home, there where the road makes a bend in front of the Maritime Museum, did a sad thought enter my mind.

&c&c&c

ARIANE

our lovely baby
larger than life
my little girl
larger than us
our little star a
galaxy

&c&c&c

Sunday May 9

Second day of paper making, my first Mother's Day. A great sadness hung over me. During the lunch break I walked through the quiet streets of the old Jordaan neighborhood and I wept. Silently.

Tuesday May 11

The continuation of the poem announced itself.

> A subtle feeling
> of knowing patience
> the faintest touch
> as felt when
> solemn meditation
> comes to an end.
>
> What's a year
> what are nine months
> growing into a longing
> the expectation present always
> patience and impatience one
> deliverance of a new galaxy
>
> A star is born
> and thus creates a void
> another unimaginable space,
> room in my heart
> with walls that dissolve
> a soap bubble
> a universe.

ॐॐॐ

Thursday May 13

"You would probably feel uncomfortable at a 'Mommy and Me' session without ARIANE." Carita said when she visited us a couple of weeks after ARIANE's birth. I imagined all the women of my pregnancy gym group with their babies and couldn't have agreed more.

"Same for the post-natal exercise class. I don't give private lessons so I suggest you go to my colleague Maria."

So, today I rode my bike to Maria's practice. Across the old town, through the south side into the green suburb of Buitenveldert. Carita's remark about Maria holding a degree in psychology as well as in the Mensendieck Science of Posture, suggested I would receive more than a private exercise lesson. And I did. After I changed into shorts and tee shirt behind a divider, Maria told me to lie on my back with bent knees on a blue rubber mat in front of a wall mirror. During a Kegel exercise combined with pelvic thrust, she asked me what happened. Flat on my back, I told her, meanwhile scanning my shape, the bulge of body mass, the slackened muscles, the pouch and I felt repelled by what I saw.

"I am so disappointed in my body. I did not give life to ARIANE. She suffocated in me."

"That she died is not your fault," Maria said. "From what I understand her death was caused by a freak accident which could have been prevented if the doctors had decided to deliver ARIANE by Caesarean section. Please don't blame yourself."

1998

Maria was most perceptive. I was seeking the cause of ARIANE's death in my own faulty body. The obstetrician's remark that a more weighty baby might have survived the traumatic delivery had started to gnaw on me. Mothers whose babies have died are so ready to blame themselves. They need to be protected, their fears should not be fed.

Thursday May 13, 1993

Cosmic Illusions, a theater production company has approached me to design for a new play by a Dutch playwright. John, the director requested me as the designer. He is still in New York.

On Tuesday I talked to the playwright at Derek Walcott's master class. A nervous, dandy, young man. He was rather full of himself... wonder boy in theater and television land, but apologized a million times for the fact that the play is not finished, that it still needs a bit of work.

I read the first draft of the script, supposedly a comedy. The comic reliefs completely escaped me, maybe they aren't even there, maybe it is me. Apart from that, I don't think I am ready to deal with the petty problems and narcissist elements of the theater. I've got to keep in mind that it is all right to refuse to do something that is not right for me!

Derek Walcott's workshop was hosted by a theater company and the master immediately divided the participants in a group of actors and one of writers. He handed out copies of Auden's Lullaby. The writers were asked to translate the poem in Dutch while preserving meter and rhythm.

The pianist at the funeral home played three lullabies for ARIANE EIRA's memorial service. Who, in this company, would relate to the lullaby the way I did, I wondered, glancing at the text through a mist.

Mister Walcott asked who wrote in verse and told those of us who don't, that the workshop would not be of interest to us. What a knock-down. Meanwhile the actors, guided by Mr. Walcott started to sing. Finally Auden's original poem was sung melodiously with now and then gospel-like eruptions from the most swinging members of the choir. I retreated. I did not feel comfortable joining the choir and felt alienated and painfully left out by Walcott's exclusive treatment of the performers.

Monday May 17

Wrote -thanks, but no thanks- note to 'Cosmic Illusions' production manager.

Saturday May 22

ANGER. Anger? Of course there was anger. I have carried the fury inside of me for months. I thought from the beginning that anger would not get me, or us anywhere; showing anger would not bring back ARIANE EIRA, our beautiful, little girl. Sadness, pain, aching search for what could not be found. Disbelief that this had to happen to us, to me. What had I done wrong? What vengeance of what power did I have to endure?

Last Sunday I broke down at the Burger King on the Leidseplein. A controlled anger, no shouting or banging of fists on Formica table tops, but rage trapped in words, spit out between bites of hamburger and chips.

"Our baby would have been alive had she been born in the States. In America they would have had me in the operation room by 6:00 P.M.. if not earlier. Here they assumed that if the diameter of her head fit my pelvic opening, I could deliver her vaginally. And then I lost my baby because she got stuck." I choked on my tears and the food. Mike patted me on my shoulders while I coughed my lungs out.

"Have some water," he handed me a paper-cup.

I gulped it down before I resumed my litany. "The OB said our baby did not have enough resilience or reserves to survive, because she was so light. But Maria told me I was the second client within a short period who lost her breech baby at that hospital. Just imagine!"

Mike let me rage. He reminded me that I was menstruating. I didn't take that as an insult.

Sunday May 23

Today I got a call from Eva, one of the organizers of our neighborhood's open studios event. She explained the concept. Participating artists will open their studios to the public during two consecutive week-ends in October. At the same time the "Oosterkerk," the church and social center of the Wittenburg city isle, will host the group exhibition where each artist will show one single piece of art.

I will ask my writer-friend Job, to let me create a paper-art/words/art-paper installation in his studio at The House of Four Winds at the tail end of the Wittenburg. His space is at street level and as large as a school room, with a twenty foot high ceiling, and the facade is all windows. A perfect place to create an instant studio.

Wednesday May 26

Eva, whom I spoke with on the phone, and her associate Fridewih came to look at my work. The latter carried a sleeping infant. They liked my work. I served tea and cookies at my work table. The baby woke up and started to fuss.

"We'll need one unframed piece, to be photographed for promotional post-cards. We'll sell packages with thirty-three cards, one of each participating artist, at the church, the starting point of the art-walk," Fridewih lifted her top, undid her bra and started to feed her baby.

"And all artists will receive five hundred cards of their own work for their own use. All that will be paid for by the organization."

"Fantastic, you can count me in."

Seeing Fridewih nurse her baby tightened my throat, I needed to leave the room. "Eva, perhaps you can help me choose a piece for the post-card? There are still some works in the little room you haven't seen."

"I also have an infant, my husband is baby sitting," Eva looked around in the already converted baby-room. "You have children too, don't you? Your place is very child friendly, great colors too."

I swallowed hard, "No, I don't have children, but I had a baby..., she is dead."

She stopped looking through a portfolio, her eyes wide open, she turned to me. "That's awful. When did this happen?"

"ARIANE EIRA was born on the eighth of January."

"Oh, my goodness," she sighed, "My daughter Mirthe was born on the fourth of January. I'm so sorry Judith"

We went back to the living-room and sat at the table.

"Judith's baby was born four days after Mirthe, ...and she died."

"I'm sorry to hear that. What happened?"

"Yes, what went wrong, do you mind telling us?"

After an hour of only women's talk, while I kept on filling their cups, they left to fetch their older children from school.

"If you wish to see a baby girl the same age as ARIANE, you're most welcome at my home," Eva turned as I let them out. "You'll probably see her anyway when you come to bring the art-work."

Sunday May 30

Cabaret performer Youp van het Hek says: "...if the child dies at childbirth, what's the use of the pregnancy? What is the use of our lives?"

I do not agree with him. My daughter has given me back my own birth rights. I am starting to understand that I am entitled to my own pain, my own grief, my own life. Until now no grief of mine could come close to the grief of Holocaust survivors. No loss could be compared. I had no right to complain, no right to feel sorry for myself, no right to be disappointed. Now I know first hand what it means to loose. When ARIANE died something in me died as well, but something important came to life. My sense of self.

1998

Like most parents, mine tried to protect me from getting hurt. Unlike other parents, they, especially my father, did not do so by creating a stable, secure home, routines I could count on, or the creation of trust.

My father's way to protect me from suffering loss was by taking away everything he presented me with. Animals; my first own dog, a black and white mutt- disappeared without explanation, so did my cocker spaniel and the dalmatian, who would come running to meet me when I'd whistle for her, half a mile away from home; ponies my dad bought for me to ride he'd sell unexpectedly. We moved from house to house like urban gypsies. Jewelry, even the chair I sat on, or my antique toys, nothing was mine to keep.

"I want you to get used to the fact that things may be taken away from you. One day you have something, the next it's gone. One day you love people, the next they're gone," my father said to me when I was only a child.

He had his reasons, he was a Holocaust survivor. One day he had a family, the next everybody was gone. One day he had a home, the next he found himself in a camp. One day he was somebody, the next he was a number.

As the child of a Holocaust survivor, I never really learned to grieve over my own hurt. A skin burn, the death of a dog, the sale of a pony, the anxiety after moving, nothing could ever compete with the pain over loosing one's whole family; a hundred thousand country-men, women and children. And after a while I started to hurt for my father's losses. Second hand experience, second hand emotion.

None of my father's precautions could prepare me for the one loss that would break the shield he had so carefully shaped. The protection shield which held up when he died, when my first marriage ended in divorce, whenever I met with adversity in my life, came down like a sugar glass window in the movies, leaving only powder when I lost ARIANE EIRA.

After I lost my baby daughter I granted myself the right to grieve for my own loss. I learned I need other people to sustain me. I learned I can rely on my mate. I learned I am not alone, but most important, I learned the value of my own feelings.

Tuesday June 1, 1993

I want to make ARIANE things. A blanky, a quilt for the bed I never got to make, a pretty smocked dress.

Thursday June 3

Maria showed me how to do a whole range of Mensendieck exercises to practice twice a day. One in particular I cannot do. I call it the -hanging belly-muscle killer- one. To do the exercise properly, I have to sit down behind my tail bone. Mine hurts. I cannot sit on or behind my tail bone at all. I forgot to tell Maria how my whole lower carriage seems to be out of alignment. I don't want to think about the pain that reminds me of the use of the forceps. Physical memory leads to mental anguish. Still, I can't deny sitting through a movie in the theater is nearly impossible. When I've been in one seated position for a while, or when I've bent over, straightening out or up takes a real effort.

Sunday June 6

Mike is learning that being married doesn't mean you have to forget yourself or that you have to follow your partner so completely that your own personality suffers or even disappears. He is learning that he can be independent and that I won't mind.

I am learning that marriage adds possibilities of strength. Being with him doesn't need to cramp my style. On the contrary, I can continue being my own person with added support from my partner.

Monday June 14

P of PERIOD. I associate the pain of cramps with ARIANE's birth. First the delivery, then the pain of loss.

I see her sweet little face in front of me, but is the memory of her face or of the photographs? I wish I could remember her features only, and her body, the actual baby. If the vivid memories during the first month after her death were too painful, the loss of them is disturbing. What I remember most are closed eyelids, lack of breath, want of color in her face. Silence, our breathing between words uttered in stunned despair, is all that remains.

Boxed memories; the colorful photographs, Dutch and American flag colors in our clothes, our snow-white baby. My weeping face, my husband's hands, cupped around the small child. A part of us, not alive, no life. Letters of response from friends and relatives and sometimes close to strangers wrapped in a silken scarf.

Mike and I are tossed around in a sea of emotions. At times we are far apart, the absence of our child a black hole between us, sucking in the whole episode of love and pain. Then again we are thrown together, merging mind, body and soul. In the new-found friendship we find togetherness. My pain known to him, the physical ordeal a shared memory.

Tuesday June 15

Yesterday I took a painting for the promotional postcard to Eva's home. She was breast feeding Mirthe. Shortly after, she put the baby to bed, while I filled out forms for the insurance and an agreement concerning the exhibition rules. After we took care of formalities and paperwork I asked to see Mirthe again. Eva took me down the stairs into the master bedroom. The baby's crib stood at the foot of her parents' bed. She was awake and

Eva picked her up and then handed her to me. We went back upstairs. A fellow artist had arrived with a painting and was waiting for Eva. In the hallway I met Eva's husband.

"Trying to steal my girl, huh," he tickled Mirthe in the fold of her knee.

The little girl, whose legs are long, as our sweetheart's undoubtedly would have been, sniffled. She had a cold and wasn't too happy. Still, she took to me and I held her for quite a while.

"You can come and baby-sit any time," Eva held out her hands to take Mirthe from me. "I believe that little thing needs clean diapers, would you like to change them? You've got to practice."

"No, thanks." What for? I thought. I feel no urge at all to take care of other people's babies.

Today I rode by the hospital. I looked up at the window from which I watched the tram stop, the red puddles. I felt a sharp pang of pain and thought: this is the place where our baby died. Tears in my eyes.

Saturday June 26

Eva told me about a woman at work, who suddenly remarked that she too was a mother. How twenty years earlier she had given birth to a baby girl. The child had died during the delivery. Her then partner and she fought to save their relationship, but alas, they lost. Years went by before she met another man with whom she thought she could share her life. That might have been, yes, but that man didn't want children. She left him. She had friends and an occasional lover, but a steady partner did not arrive until she was middle aged. Over the hill and no longer able to conceive. Life with her current husband was pleasant. Their relationship was a quiet one. Not boring. Simple conflicts still erupted, but with the settling down of hormones, peace arrived. And, oh well, babies she could see as much as she liked.

I wonder whether our story will be like this woman's in twenty years, or will our relationship survive? Each day we're confronted with the true difficulty of communication between man and woman.

Sunday June 27

Mike and I went on an outing today. We took the bus from the Central Station to Broek in Waterland, a picturesque village just north of Amsterdam. We ate pancakes the size of hub-caps at the old pancake house. Mike chose bacon and thick sugar-cane syrup. I chose apple, dusted with powdered sugar and cinnamon. Afterwards, we circled the pond in the center of the old village. The water, smooth like a mirror, rippled here and there where ducks paddled around. The houses are mostly built of wood, with subtle touches on the boards, decorative reliefs or borderlines. Walking on cobblestone roads, through narrow streets felt somewhat like walking through the set of a ghost town. With one house in particular, I could not resist the urge to take a few steps to the side of the lot, to see if there was a real three dimensional house behind the green, painted, boarded front. We walked by a replica of an ancient house. Marjolein's house and her attached studio were destroyed by a fire. The new house built up from the ashes of the monumental building, is painted antique ox-blood red, instead of the more common and demure gray. At a whim, I waved at the crocheted lace curtain that covers the glass in the front door. To our surprise the door opened and Marjolein invited us in. We have known each other for a long time but had not been in touch lately. We hugged and I introduced Mike.

In the small kitchen adjacent to the entrance, Marjolein put on a kettle of water. "The fire occurred just before a major exhibition," she said. "All of my latest work, my private collection of favorite pieces, my documentation and library was destroyed." She placed three Japanese cups on a tray. "And everything else, all of my and my daughter's belongings were gone in no time at all. We were lucky to have gotten out."

"How did it happen? What woke you up?" I asked.

"Our neighbor Hans came home late after a gig, noticed the fire and he screamed and yelled and banged on the door to wake us up."

She rebuilt house and studio, making the most economic use of the space and now has more room than before.

The way she talked, about losing her documentation of twenty-five years of art-work, reminded me of my state without baby to account for the fact, that I am a mother indeed.

Marjolein rinsed out the Japanese teapot, scooped in loose tea leaves and poured on the steaming water. Taking the tray with cups and teapot, she showed us her studio. Sliding wooden panels either open up or close off the work-space from the rest of the house. These six foot panels double as work-boards. A work in process, a water-color on a large sheet of paper was pinned onto one of the sliding doors. We followed her up the stairs to the loft-living-room where we sat down, Japanese style on pillows at a low table.

Marjolein presented me with a stack of cards, reproductions of her work; tulip abstracts, an homage to our country. The night after the fire, sleepless in a hospital bed, she realized that a card publisher, the owner of Art Unlimited, had ten slides of her latest work in his possession. Apart from work in private collections, this was all that remained of a twenty five year career.

Starting all over again, from scratch, without anything from the past to aid you in remembering who you were and are, is unsettling and inevitable after a devastating fire. You're back at the drawing board without any material of reference. Marjolein created an inspirational clean slate by erecting this new place. A space to house the arts. Compared to her I am still searching among the cinders.

Tuesday June 29

Too awake to sleep, I got up and watched Oprah. Theme: infertility or childless marriages. One woman said she had spent all her days at the cemetery after her baby's death.

"Couples often don't make it through the tragedy of losing a baby, because they take their anger out on their spouses, or because they don't talk," remarked the show's professional adviser. "Sometimes," she added, "The loss brings people closer together."

The other day, right before falling asleep, I remembered the delivery: how ARIANE was stuck. I turned and twisted in bed with agony. I did not tell Mike, who was at my side, reading a book, but he rubbed my back and comforted me until I drifted off.

Thursday July 8

Today ARIANE EIRA six months.

Saturday July 31

"Always concentrate on your self, your own role, instead of getting on Mike's case. Most of your aggravation is hidden anger," Joanita said when I told her I get aggravated with Mike for just hanging, doing nothing.

Watched *She's Having a Baby*. I saw the film with Kevin Bacon and Elizabeth McGovern while I was pregnant. I did not recall the baby being in breech position!

"A complication, the baby is in breech position and the head is caught... we'll do all we can."

The doctors in the movie performed a C-section and both mother and child lived.

"It's a boy Mrs.Briggs, it's a boy."

Shouldn't the obstetrician have been at the hospital, at my delivery earlier, sooner?

Later in bed we spooned, the pillow nearly suffocated me. I recalled the six pillows I needed to get comfortable in bed when I was pregnant; the awkwardness and discomfort especially during the night. Although I cannot, or do not want to remember what the labor pains were like, I know the onset resembled menstrual cramps. I know labor was painful and hard and there is no compensation for the hardship, having lost ARIANE. They say women forget the pain once they have their baby in their arms. Forgetting the pain helps them to go through it all again with the next child. The pain I remember makes me not ever want to have to go through labor and delivery again.

I miss my perfectly healthy baby.

Monday August 16

I find it impossible to talk with my mother about our loss. She has not referred to ARIANE since she looked at the photographs on Mike's birthday in March.

I don't say anything either. I am incapable of asking for compassion. Once bitten, twice shy? If only she'd give me the initial -A-, the way she uses -C- for the feared cancer, the letter supposedly explaining what somebody she knows is suffering from. The sole letter standing for the whole arsenal of words that may not cover the pain inflicted by the devastating disease. Think of the hurt of the patient whose disposition is brought back to a mere letter, probably accompanied by a sideways glance and then whispers or silence. The latter is all I get from my mother. My loss is not even adorned by a letter. How appropriate it would be to pronounce the capitol -A- with all the force, carrying love and pain and compassion, a breath can take. When I say -A- and I think of ARIANE my vocal cords tremble and I know that's what vocal cords do. Trembling is in their nature, the resonance of life. The first letter of my daughter's name -A-sung with my throat wide open, releases the agony trapped in my body and when continued the sound spirals back toward my heart, leaving me with nothing but a fresh breath to take and bewilderment over the emptiness or openness after such meditation. So give me an -A- Mama. Talk to me about my daughter's death. Don't fear that remembering my baby will upset me, don't be afraid of mentioning her name. What hurts is blanketing.

Tuesday August 17

Woke up at 4:00 with a headache. Got up to take a painkiller. Am trying to work for the exhibition, but I spend more time sorting material, throwing out old correspondence. Shredding a lot of paper, which I plan to recycle.

Yesterday evening I went to the twenty-first birthday and house-warming party for Tina's daughter, Sally. I did not look forward to seeing people I know mostly from social functions, people I meet once or twice each year, who might know about ARIANE, but whom I had not seen yet. I talked myself into going. I have known Sally since she was three weeks old. I wanted to help celebrate this important day. I went early to Sally's new apartment so that I'd have some time with Tina before the others would arrive. While she fixed party food I visited with her in the kitchen.

Sally's father entered the apartment with his latest wife. He kissed me, but did not say a word to acknowledge my loss. Inappropriate at his daughter's birthday perhaps? Soon the apartment filled up with family and friends. All the chairs were taken and many guests stood around talking. I found a place on the couch in the living room and enjoyed a conversation with near strangers, people I had seen at other family occasions. Then Jacky, an old acquaintance arrived with her teenage son. She sat down beside me. We chatted about the old times and she filled me in on the work she does nowadays.

"What about you Judith?" Without waiting for my reply, Jacky looked me straight in the eye and said: "You've lost your spark. That's not good. You know what I'm talking about, you used to be sparkling. You can get that back, if only you work on it."

I was perplexed. All I could come up with was "Oh, really." I excused myself and went to the bathroom. Then I walked around to find the birthday girl to say goodbye. Tina and I embraced. "That woman told me I lost my spark," I nearly cried in my girl-friend's ear.

"I know," Tina, holding my arms, pushed me away just enough so she could look me in the eye. "She didn't know about ARIANE, I have filled her in. She is real sorry about your loss and also about what she said. She did not mean to hurt you." We hugged again. Sally squeezed herself between her mother and me and the three of us embraced before I said goodbye.

Friday August 20

Oh, a room of one's own! I wish I had not given up my art-studio before I went to the States. Mike has a hard time getting used to my work method. He says that I am not disciplined. When he does not see any progress, he thinks nothing is going on. I have difficulty making him understand that everything I do is work related. And a large part of the work is going on in my mind. When I design sets or costumes, a lot of the work takes place in my head. Sometimes weeks go by before I make sketches. Hardly anything is purely entertainment. Newspapers, movies, books, conversations they can all supply inspiration.

Not having a proper studio to work in doesn't help much. Without solitude there is no creative process or progress. Surely Picasso did not have to explain all this, he probably did not have the problems I have.

Thursday August 26

I discussed the perils of not having a live-in studio with Joanita. With Mike working as a stage and studio technician, he's likely to be home during the day, when I need my solitude. She advised me to rearrange the furniture so that I'll be able to work at home. Immediately after the counseling session, I masked the glass kitchen door with paper and brought in Papa's tall, oak desk to barricade the door to the hallway.

In the evening I made a linoleum-cut of a whore in the window of a 17th century canal house, number one on my list for the series WINDOW SHOPPING IN AMSTERDAM. Mike is intrigued by the hookers in the windows, but from a distance. He regards the hookers as an exotic element of Holland.

Wednesday, I worked on watercolor and colored ink melted into wet mounted paper; creeks of color meandered around oil pastel, slick like melted butter. I wanted to put the essence of our child in the painting. I danced with my brushes, swirling in the narrow space between hollow core table and couch. Mike made hamburgers for dinner. He is in a good mood, happy even. No television. To bed early. This morning I woke up inspired.

Saturday August 28

At the cremation Jeanette said: "With ARIANE gone, part of you died. When a child dies, a part within the mother dies as well." How true that is; I feel that hole. When your child dies, you need to take extra care of yourself, and let others assist you with that. You need to be nourished and nurtured.

I have a special bond with ARIANE EIRA. She is somewhere, somewhere in the universe, her spirit is connected with mine. The eternal umbilical cord, the symbiotic yet unobtainable, romantic love. Forever one.

Losing your child pushes you further on the path of no return, like losing your virginity. There is no way back. With each lost love, something in you dies and you gain steps on the path of no return. When your baby dies, you lose your innocence.

❧❧❧

OXYGEN

I live without the praise
for somebody else's being
I can not make mistakes
all expectations back to zero
mother
only in the practice of delivering
a healthy baby girl,but
for the lack of OXYGEN I wonder:
is blood without O....O
still thicker than water?

❧❧❧

LOSS

When the blood came
daddy said: "Now you are a woman." I cried
over my childhood **LOSS**
When the man died who named me after a woman of
substance; the queen of red hot lava, the blood mother, there
was nothing left to do, but to search for the next man who'd
crown me **LOSS**
When I saved my virginity,
for the special one, it meant so little **LOSS**
When a parent is taken, not by death, but for a lack of further
expectation, with a mind of her own that fits no other reality
than the one that is her's alone **LOSS**
When I never saw the color of my baby's eyes. Never saw her
nostrils flare, nor ever heard her cry **LOSS**
When bereft of motherhood, but for the
practice of delivering **LOSS**
When after nine months of waiting the expectation
is cut short **LOSS**
When I am not in my right mind **LOSS**

&ε &ε &ε

Monday August 30

I consulted the *I CHING*. Meditation help for the ART-WORK.
Threw my three copper pennies and got oracle 31: Tension.
Success if you keep to your course and remain receptive to others.
Followed by 62: Smallness in Excess. Take on small tasks and
shy away from large ones. Attempt no major undertakings. You
can be successful and happy in your minor attempts.
Maintain common everyday attitudes. Express sorrow, not
fatalism or piety. Be yourself, know who you are.

Wednesday September 1

Yesterday, I painted enormous letters with a broad house painters
brush in diluted Sumi ink on 65x50 centimeter sheets of paper.
I spelled the words B L O O D and L O S S on separate sheets,
blotted them with newsprint and then wrote on them with a
crown pen in full strength ink.Writing my poems in that manner

gives tremendous satisfaction. While working on my lettering, a song by the English band THE POLICE, "Message in a Bottle," made its way into my mind.I replaced part of the lyrics: "I sent an s.o.s.to the world," by my own.

☙☙☙

IOU

I've got an IOU from the hospital
Had my IUD removed
Pregnant right away
Had a healthy baby girl
She died on the way

☙☙☙

After the *I CHING*, I turned to the *Book of Runes*.

The issue: MY ART-WORK/POETRY. I drew the stone with the symbol INGUZ. This stands for fertility. New Beginnings. INGUZ embodies the need to share my poetry and art-work; a search after feedback and appreciation, recognition and understanding.

The RUNES tell me I have the strength to make the works known. Completion is crucial. INGUZ signals my emergence from depression, from a rut.

Saturday September 4

I lost six pounds of the eighteen! And that was before Jan the owner of the fitness club took me on as his personal prodigy. He was unaware of my accomplishment.

"You've gained some weight," he whispered in my ear when he saw me again after my long absence. "What happened?"

"I had a baby," I said blushing.

"How old is.. what is it, a he or a she, now?"

"She died."

Jan the muscle man turned to mush. His broad neck stood out bright red against the white of his t-shirt, his ears joined in coloration. The face of that great, big, former weight lifting champion flooded pink with compassion. He hugged me against his still hard body, the waist band of his blue sweat pants pressed against my breasts.

"I am so sorry," he took a moment, then collected himself. "You're going to be okay. You're style is good. We're gonna work on repetitions, so you'll lose weight and won't build up too much muscle. Now let me see how you do those curls. Fine. Three times twelve to start with." He winked at me as he walked off, hitting his thighs with his towel. "You're gonna be fine."

Sunday September 5

Mike and I bumped into one of the Afro-American-Indian-Jewish Christmas Twins in front of their eclectic coffee shop in the Utrechtse dwarsstraat. He wore one of their signature hand-crafted rainbow sweaters. I waved.

"How are you?" he shouted.

"Fine. How are things going with you?" I turned in my step. He made a happy grimace: "How is your baby?"
I looked up at the clear blue sky and spreading my arms I sang: "She is a star."

"Good," he smiled broadly. Approaching us he looked at me carefully: "Now are you who I think you are?"

"I don't know," I shrugged. Mike just grinned.

"No," his twin stepped outside the coffee shop.
Now they were both standing in front of us, even their Mohawk haircuts identical. Number one brother apologized raising his eyebrows high and shaping his lips in a round: "Oh, I thought you were house-sitting next door."

"No," all three of us sang. Laughing we shook hands and said goodbye.

୬୬୬

"How's the baby?" "She's a star."
When my baby died it left me empty inside. Young
mothers, they all think I wish to share their babies, which
surely I don't. I cannot bare their energy, or the lack of it,
both brilliance and dullness of the parents' thought.
My child is in darkness and a star, and therefore LIGHT,
she cannot compete with bright eyes or dirty diapers and
neither can I. She is always present, although I do not carry
her around. Some see her, for something is missing in my
eye, a spark which she took,
my star.

Monday September 6

My friend Marjan classified the Dutch-Delft-Blue style patch-
work blocks I've started as boring.

"Handicraft, needlework," she sniffed with contempt, You've
become a real housewife haven't you."

In her eyes I have lost my ability to be creative, to make great
art. What does she know? So I'm feeling blue. The Blues is only
the beginning. Serenade in blue and brights. I imagine
combining the blue with shaggy green and the bright colors of
the tulip fields, red, yellow, orange and purple. A serenade to
ARIANE EIRA.

I plan to make an installation in Job's space called BLOOD
LOSS.

An advertisement in the local paper caught my attention. A
graphic artist offered etching classes. She agreed to give me a
few private lessons, just me. I went today and worked on my
first plate since high school. Chicken and egg, a vertical cartoon
with images depicting the life span of a hen.

Tuesday September 7

Early this evening I met with the other artists participating in
the open studio event. We had to assemble packages, a total of
thirty-three different post-cards, representations of our work.
One of the women was heavy with child. I would have liked to
talk to her, but was afraid of her question: "Do you have
children?" What would I have answered? Can you tell a woman
ready to deliver that your perfectly healthy baby died? I think
you cannot. I cannot.

The front of the sleeve that holds the cards has a reduced
image of the poster for the exhibition (it doubles as an invitation
card). I like the design, but it makes an Asian impression on me
and I don't think that's suitable for my work, or even this group
show. I'll create my own invitation. We all went home with
three of the assembled packages and more than 500 cards of our
own work. I'm delighted with my post-cards. When I turned in
the work to be photographed, I needed to give a title. Since
most of that lively, colorful series, which the work was part of,
was made while I lived in Paris at Rue de la Reunion, I named
the painting *Reunion*.

Friday September 10

Feel totally powerless and yet a rush of nervous energy makes me restless, shakes my inner self. The issue at hand is US, Mike and I together. Or is it my state of powerlessness, I?

When I consult the RUNES the oracle MANNAZ, the Self (in reverse) tells me: Strive to live the ordinary life in a non-ordinary way.

If you feel blocked, do not turn to others, but look inside, in silence, for the enemy of your progress.

How can I when not being in control makes me so nervous?

ೇೇೇ

ROCK

I feel a rock behind my eyes
when I squeeze them tightly, tears
more than reluctantly make their
sullen appearance and already the physical pain/
hurt is gone. Have I wept too much or enough.
I need only a tear to continue.
The clear water drop, polishing the surface of stone,
the calm of nature's cycle, reflected in dapper green,
growing without soil, thriving on minuscule
mineral traces.
I feel a rock behind my eyes

ೇೇೇ

Monday September 13

Tired, so tired. Have decided that I can show my pain and growth in my show, since I want to share, not hurt. In dealing with the pain of losing a child, can you be CANDID when sharing the anguish with other MOTHERS as well? Be candid, be fair, be blunt, be frank about the loss of a baby, your baby.

CANDID

About death of your baby, losing blood, losing virginity,
losing innocence.
BLOOD LOSS EXHIBITION-ISM
How CANDID can one be?
U-T
CAN-DID
CAN-U-T
HOW-CAN-U-T-BE
About life, about death, about blood.
CANDID bright, white, fr. candere to shine, glow; akin to
LGk kandaros ember]
1:white (r flames)
2:free from bias, prejudice, or malice: FAIR (a ~observer)
3a: marked by honest sincere expression
b:indicating or suggesting sincere honesty and absence of
deception.
4: Relating to photography of subjects acting naturally or
spontaneously without being posed (~picture)
syn see FRANK ant evasive
FAIR- be FAIR about losing a baby
BLUNT- may be BLUNT about losing a baby
FRANK- can be FRANK about losing a baby
WAR, DEATH, CASUALTIES, ILLNESS. All that people are
willing to talk about, but BIRTH, LIFE, DEATH you're supposed to be silent about. In dealing with the pain of losing a
child, can you be CANDID to share it with other MOTHERS?
"Never ever say a negative thing to a pregnant woman."
That's what I learned at an early age. If you are the cause of a
miscarriage, you may be sued.
PLANNING FOR EXHIBITION-ISM-JOB
I've been making art-work: trying as I might to find out what I
should do. Why? To have new work to present at the
EXHIBITION-ISM.
HOW CANDID CAN ONE BE? EXHIBITION-ISM. SO YOU
LIKE TO WATCH? AM I MORE PERSONAL THAN THE
CRAZY MOTHERS OR A MOTHER IN FORMER
YUGOSLAVIA?

ᘒ ᘒ ᘒ

Tuesday September 14

Sunday we took the train to Utrecht where we rented bicycles at the station. We had bought a train-bike pass, which included a tour map of the area. Obediently, we rode to the forested Lage Vuursche, Soest and Soesterberg, Den Dolder and Zeist carefully reading the instructions on the map. We passed meadows with cows chewing the cud, scenes straight off an old Dutch master. It was a balmy day. Near Soesterberg we stepped off our bikes and parked them against the foot-high wooden poles that mark off the bike path. We stretched out in the sweet-smelling heather protected from the wind by oak trees and shared an apple. The insects were buzzing, other than that not a sound disturbed the quiet. Even occasional groups of cyclists honored the serenity of nature by keeping their volume down. After our break, we followed the designated bike-path for another mile. Instead of continuing on the sea-shell covered trail, we turned left onto a farm road, just in time to see a cow give birth with the assistance of a farmer. The man used a contraption to push at the mother's belly and at the same time pull at the legs of the calf with a rope. The calf was in breech. Poor mother. We were not the only ones to stop. I heard a young girl say to her companions: "Let's go on, I don't want to watch that, it is dirty."

Sunday September 19

"You're trying to recreate ARIANE," Mike leaned on my work table pointing at my ink drawings "I've seen you struggle with those ultra sound copies for days now; can't you just take them for what they are?"

He was right. I was trying to make art out of the one image we have of ARIANE still alive, in my belly.

And what about all those weeks of making paper out of discarded correspondence; the sheets pressed between magazine pages are piling up, but what am I going to do with them?

The whole paper making business started out of frustration. I did not know how to bring ARIANE back. Recycling letters, correspondence an essential part of my design business, seemed the next best thing to do.

Mike's remark brought forth the solution I have been struggling to find. I have made a collage of an enlarged photo of myself, the ultra sound image and Sumi ink.

Finally I'm freed to make drawings on the recycled paper. *We're all ants in the eyes of the Gods*, is what I call the series.

During the day I work on my presentation for the show. In the evening I draw ant-like creatures in a world of their own, the environment presents itself to me through the rough surface of the paper. I feel productive. My creativity has been unleashed.

Saturday September 25

Job gave me the key to his office. An important moment for both of us. We each have the best intentions, still I am curious to see whether this arrangement will work out. After all he is used to solitude and I will be present in person and with my art. He will become part of my installation.

Mike used the bottom part of the baby carriage to bring over the work tables and practically everything else I could not manage on my bicycle.

"If you're not going to use that cart anymore I'd like to have it," one of our neighbors told him. She delivers flyers and brochures, hauling the paperwork from house to house in a grocery bag on wheels. I think I'd rather see a baby in our carriage.

One of my friends called after she received the invitation.

"Very deep, very deep. Reunion, I know, it has everything to do with the loss of your baby." (!)

⚊⚊⚊

LOST

In mourning I tear up/ ten years of correspondence/ and
attempt to recycle with the need to recreate/ The result a
disappointing/ grayish matter, not the/ silky rough or rough
silken/ paper which breathes on its own account:
handle with care. A chlorine smell lingers on/ as in-erasable
words drift/ without direction or reason/ breakers interfering/
with poetic flow With this lack of function/ I'm only facing
shredded paper illusions/ incapable of competition/
with the sharpest pain/ the merely unmentionable

LOSS

Wednesday September 29

Nicole came up from Paris, she had an appointment with a gallery owner in town, to show her port-folio to. I'm sure she'll do well. Her prints are like the interior of her home, playful, filled with color, amusing shapes and tremendous accessibility. Nicole works without linear perspective, every movement in her work takes place on one plane, filling a whole sheet with action.We met for lunch at the Luxembourg Grand Cafe´on the Spui. She sat waiting for me at the reading table in the lively and open front section.I suggested a more quiet table in the rear. Nicole looked fragile, the way I remembered her. Nervous, unsure, her smile a quiver of the lips. Against her trade mark ultramarine clothes, her skin shone translucent like thin milk. Lanky and angelic with azure eyes and delicate ash-blond curls she resembles the figures in her own Chagall-like art work.

She talked about the boys, Guy and Julian and how well they're doing. Guy got his first paid-for assignment, designing the cover for a book. When I asked her about his health, her eyes flooded, she trembled all over. My hand felt pudgy and damp touching her lean fingers. I stroked them while she sobbed.

Guy, who has muscular dystrophy had reached another phase in his illness. He is no longer able to eat solid food. All of a sudden, while having fun with his friends he seemed to choke. Now he could take in only liquid food. He and Julian had gone to Denmark by van, stocked up with highly scientific mixes containing all the nutrients his body needs.

"He is so brave, he jokes about having the same diet as astronauts." Nicole smiled through her tears. "He continues working on his computer, creating music and now the assignment..," she dried her tears with a dainty handkerchief. "He and Julian went to Berkeley this summer. They were put up in handicapped student housing and he had the time of his life..." She started weeping again.

"You are brave as well. I understand how hard it must be to see your child suffer. I am amazed by your art-work, your family's "joie de vivre," you are such a wonderful family, all of you working so hard on making life a worthwhile experience."

She nodded, but the look on her face was of defeat. For once she had let down the shield of optimism in front of a relative stranger. She seemed embarrassed and relieved at the same time.

After we finished a second coffee, we said goodbye and kissed. I wished her success in her negotiations with the gallery. Her lips quivered their uneasy smile. I watched her walk away while I unlocked my bike. She never looked back.

Wednesday October 6

On the way from our apartment to Job's studio, my chest tightened, as if my heart was clenched by a fist. Arteries, tense like bony fingers, clawed my neck. My throat dry, left raw by a silent scream from deep within, refused to answer my urge to swallow. A scorching pain behind my eyes where tears seem to have dried up, made blinking an ordeal.

What is this anxiety about? Fear of creating, fear of being by myself, on my own. Fear of starting all over again? Fear of facing my fears?

Last night we went to see *In the Line of Fire*. After the movie we had a showarma sandwich at the hole in the wall across from the theater.

"You look like a bum with your hair growing out like that, You need a haircut. And why don't you shave off that silly beard?"

Later I apologized. Only now do I realize that my good looking husband let go of his appearance because he is in mourning. And I am acting nasty because I feel rotten. Taking my misery out on him.

Friday October 8
ARIANE EIRA nine months.

The floor plan of the studio measures 30 x 30 feet, the walls are 20 feet tall. The facade wall is all window, with the entrance door on the right hand side (when you're facing the building from the outside). If you divide the space in four equal squares, the library and open kitchen are in the far left hand corner. Job has allowed me to move his work tables into that section during the hours that people are expected to visit my exhibition. In the far right hand corner is a loft, where I am showing my large acrylics of the nineteen-eighties. On the ground floor is the bathroom and a storage area. In front of the curtains behind which Job hides his easy chair and vacuum cleaner, I have built an installation. When the visitors enter from the street, they are channeled into the BABY BLUES ROOM. I papered flats with colored funny pages of the Los Angeles Times that show Rick Kirkman and Jerry Scott's BABY BLUES cartoon. Then, around the corner are my black painted phrases on top of the colorful cartoon back-ground: "When a child dies, a part within the mother dies as well."

On the white interior wall that backs the kitchen area, I hung STARLIGHT, the collage. My two worktables are in the middle of the right hand space, covered with my hand-made paper and drawing series IN THE EYES OF THE GODS WE ARE ANTS. The newest watercolor and oil pastel works are on the white wall to the right of the entrance door, the series of six REUNION works hang on the left hand wall, together with my six oil pastel self-portraits. I'll have portfolios with unframed work on Job's worktables for guests to look through. The metal frame of the sculpture from my performance THE ESTRANGER stands naked, hollow, that is, without costume, in front of the windows. Next to it the card-rack filled with my own post-cards. I am pleased.

Tuesday October 19

Sunny day, a blue sky with high white puffs. Yesterday was stormy. Clouds raced each other toward an unknown finish. I followed them as far as I could through the tall windows of Job's office. Two more days and I will have to vacate this space. The open studio was a success. I am back in the saddle. I feel great knowing I can still push on when necessary. Job gave me more than time and room when he let me set up the installation a week before the opening. I needed to experience again the luxury of working in a space other than my home. My relationship with Mike certainly has improved. I came here as often as possible. Job knew I'd be here when he was working elsewhere, but he was always surprised to find me when he arrived. He told me on several occasions that there was no need for me to leave after his arrival. Neither of us can work at home with our mates around, but we have no problem continuing our projects when together. One of those days together, I wrote my lamentations, the poems for and about ARIANE EIRA written in Sumi ink on a roll of Japanese rice paper.

When I lost the urge to continue, I cut the paper and attached the ends to small wooden dowels. Rolled up it looks like a mini Torah. I hung it next to the STARLIGHT collage.

I sold some mixed media pieces, ANT drawings and quite a few post-cards. Two pastels, abstracts of neighborhood scenes, will stay with Job. They seem to be at home in his studio. A small offering to thank him for his hospitality.

1998

The Open Studios project provided a welcome incentive to use my creativity again. The idea of sharing my experience with an audience, greater than our direct circle of friends, inspired me to write a series of poems. Which in turn let to works of art. I hoped to convey to people how remembering a lost loved one is part of the healing process, because I knew how hushing up could hurt.

Thursday October 21

Mike and I are planning for our return to the States. He doesn't want to try and have another baby here. He wants to go back to America where he feels more secure about work, and yes, about the care I'll receive.

ARIANE was on my mind when I woke up this morning. I thought of her brother or sister, our next child, yet to be conceived. The next one will live. I know for sure. I will project that thought as much as I can. And what if my wishes won't come true? Won't I miss the protective force of the calculated fear? We'll see. I know I can grow strong again. But the next baby will live. The next baby should be bigger, so that he or she cannot swim around in my belly and get into breech. If the baby decides to go in breech, then I wish to have a Caesarean. If he or she is head down, not too big-headed and I'm large enough, natural childbirth, please.

Tuesday November 2

For months I've been stiff and sore when getting up in the morning and after having sat in one position for a while. That is less so now. Still, when I lift my knees high, a jarring sound of bone on bone, tells me there might be something out of place in my hip sockets.

Monday November 8

Today is ARIANE EIRA's 10th month birthday. I recall her little face, the small body. I told Mike: her birth seems so long ago. Tears are far away today. My little girl, my bigger than life love. I do feel sad. Yes, I recognize this lost feeling.

Wednesday November 10

My birthday. Today I am thirty-eight. I woke up in my dream, to find Mike close at my side and myself very big. I wore a blouse with an avalanche of frills and I had to lift them to see I was pregnant. Someone, a nurse, said the baby was a cry-baby. Mike told me that he had sat on my pee-pee hole to keep the kid inside of me, to keep him from falling out.

"It is a boy," he said, "And I don't know much about a baby's anatomy, but I'm sure I felt his nose." So this baby really wanted to come out head first. In the half sleep that followed, I started thinking about contractions and I heard myself huffing and puffing. I woke up thinking about ARIANE and got scared. I wrapped my legs and arms around Mike. He wanted to shake me off, but I said: "I need you."

"Okay," he answered.

As a symbol, the image of the nose in my dream, stands for somebody (the child) coming in between us...

Tuesday November 16

Today we started the visa procedure. I will have to immigrate now that I am married to an American.

Pauline and Ryan, who weren't in town to see my exhibition, came over for dinner and to see the remainder of my newest work. Ryan questioned the value of my new collection.

"Whatever happened to the career minded girl in the power suit?" He looked at my paper art and the ANTS series with slight contempt. "If you make a whole lot of that, you could sell it as wallpaper."

I felt stung. Here I was, glad to have managed so far and this man, whom I thought was a friend with feelings of compassion, puts down my efforts. He insulted and hurt me. He is full of appreciation for an old boyfriend of mine who makes realistic paintings of celebrities. I wonder whether he is impressed by the art or by the names that go with the faces. While he and Pauline have the largest collection of my work in the Netherlands, I suddenly don't count anymore. But, let's face it, there is nothing wrong with designing wallpaper.

Tuesday December 14

Hanna invited us to have dinner with her at an Italian restaurant last night.

"You can't move to the States without your possessions. I'll pay for the move." Waving our objections away with her glass of wine, she spilled some drops onto the table cloth. "Oops, good thing it's white wine." She dabbed the spot with her napkin, "Just get an estimate from a respectable moving company and I'll pick up the bill. Okay?" She lifted her glass, "Say yea to a sunny future in America, people."

"I'll toast to that," Mike lifted his glass as well.

I accepted only after Hanna agreed to choose a piece of art in return for her generosity. The least I can do.

"I'd be delighted," she said.

Once, my most cherished belongings fit in a cardboard shoe box. Found objects; bottle caps, a carefully folded paper napkin, things worthless to my father, became valuable to me. I hung the box, the opening sideways, on a nail next to my bed, my private treasure chest. As an adult, I have schlepped boxes filled with books from one apartment to the next. I have set up a close to professional kitchen and accumulated a nice collection of art supplies, but apart from the functional metal shelves I never really invested in furniture. I do have Papa's antique oak clerk's desk and thanks to an inheritance a mahogany linen chest and writing table. No longer do my treasures fit in a shoe box, I have enough belongings to fill a large box truck. And thanks to Hanna I won't have to leave anything behind.

Monday December 20

When Mike is at work, I can hardly wait for the time he'll be back. When he is later than I expect, I think of the worst. I worry incessantly about his well being when he is not around. Ironic, for months I wanted him to go out, leave me alone and now I miss him. Melancholy feelings about leaving Amsterdam combined with the hurt over losing ARIANE weigh heavily on me.

Thursday December 23

Last night, while I was taking a shower, I recalled the days before last year's Christmas; the midwives, trying to turn our baby. Oh, such sorrow.

When I told Mike, he said: "Now is not last year."

"Please don't come up with explanations or solutions, just let me tell you how I feel."

"Okay, I'll try, but it's hard for me to merely listen when I know you're feeling bad. I like to solve the problem."

"I know, but it doesn't work that way. Let's just try and be nice for ourselves and each other. And let's not be so stingy to save all our money for our big move, let's spend some on fun things.

"Like going for a boat-ride on the canals at night when the city is lit up, or see a movie."

"Yes or go to an exhibition and have a nice meal out some time."

Doing something nice for myself means doing something creative, perhaps make a little ARIANE chap book with poems.

Sunday December 26

Christmas went by quietly, no guests, no big dinner, nothing.

Saturday January 1, 1994

Mama stayed with us for New Year's eve. We ate and drank, played Scrabble, watched television and at midnight we admired the fireworks.

We look back on the past year with sadness and onward with hope. We will be leaving for the United States at the end of this month. Off for a fresh start. I have relative peace with my mother's restrictions and cherish what she did give me over the years. She was always there for me when I was a child. She encouraged my creativity, taught me love for nature and language and respect for the environment and all creatures in it. Our relationship is so enmeshed, she doesn't want to see me hurt, for she doesn't want to feel the pain herself.

Saturday January 8

ARIANE EIRA in memoria.I've decided to always capitalize the name of my daughter. We lit three candles. One for each: Mike and me and our ARIANE EIRA STAR CHILD UNTOUCHABLE.

⅌ ⅌ ⅌

Sunday January 9
In memoria ARIANE

⅌ ⅌ ⅌

It is January the ninth and
it was hard to locate grieve
Anger Yes Nastiness in words
Wondering what would
happen one year after

Nine months and zero - one
from zero to nine and
again until three months later
a year has gone by

Expectations of the birthday
celebration of life and death
when nothing changes or arrives
all directions are lost
and without that we drift

⅌ ⅌ ⅌

Tuesday January 18

We took the pram to the health care center and told the receptionist she could give it away to people who needed a carriage for their baby. Not for delivering flyers, I thought.
"You don't want any money?"
"No, make somebody happy."
On Saturday and Sunday we held an -Everything Must Go Moving Sale- and sold most everything we had not packed to take with us to America to friends or acquaintances and some strangers who were attracted by my ad in the paper. What was left we put in plastic bags at the curb for the Morning Star, Amsterdam's unofficial recycler.

Friday January 21

On Wednesday we said goodbye to Mama. She did not make a fuss. Strong, everything under control, as usual.

"I will miss you, but I won't try to keep you here when you say your future lies elsewhere."

1998

"After the death of a loved one, moving is the second most important reason for depression." Joanita's warning remark did not make much of an impression on either of us. Mike was going back to his familiar territory and I thought twenty years of traveling back and forth between Europe and America had prepared me for the move across the ocean. Little did I know about being an immigrant. I had been a frequent guest before, but always with a secure base in Amsterdam and plenty of friends to fall back on.

On New-Year's eve I looked forward to our fresh start and a fresh start it would be.

🔊

HEALING

We made our first home in America in the Texas hill country, just outside Wimberley, a small town thirty-five winding miles outside of Austin. We rented a blue wooden house, near Old Baldy, one of the Twin Sister Mounts, on the edge of Wood Creek, a retirement resort built around a golf course.

Two years earlier we had spent a night in a cabin at the Wood Creek Lodge, less than a quarter mile from our new home. Back then, I was already smitten by the aquiferous environment; rolling hills dressed in army fatigues; the ocher earth mottled with dark-green juniper brush, rust and forest green of cedar and mesquite and the live-oak trees draped in grayish green moss. I remembered the air, aromatic with burning cedar, sweet honey, or the spicy fumes of back-yard barbecue. Mike had showed me the quaint western town and took me to a restaurant with a deck overlooking the meandering Cypress creek.

"I would like to live here sometime," I said while we waited at a rustic table for our hamburgers.

That summer of 1992 we swam at Hamilton's pool near Austin; a fine example of the aquifer's caved-in beauty. In Wimberley, Mike showed me Blue Hole, and Jacob's Well. We drove along or crossed the Blanco River. An unruly waterway, in some places wide and powerful, in others more a river of boulders, rocks and pebbles, and water an afterthought.

It was in Wimberley that I saw my first fireflies. Hundreds, perhaps thousands hanging closely together creating a cloud of diffuse light.

I could not have dreamt we would find a house as swiftly as we did. All we had to do was check the message board outside Country Boys, the local grocery store, to see the advertisement.

It read: Available immediately, one-bedroom house on $1/2$ acre, large living-room, fire-place, and sun-room.

The next morning we met with Red, the owner. He drove up in an old green pick-up truck loaded with fire-wood. He undoubtedly still wore the same size blue jeans he did when he was eighteen, the waistband snug under a taut beer belly. The little hair he had left was the color of carrots.

"I'll be happy to work with you guys," he gave us a set of keys in exchange for our check.

What -working with us- meant became clear in the months to follow. I saw him again a couple of weeks after we had moved in, when he backed his truck into our drive-way unannounced. In the bed, under the blue tarp sat two enormous chairs upholstered in a bold floral print. I saw him coming and opened the door before he could knock.

"Good morning Judith I have some nice chairs for you," he wiped his brow and shiny skull with a red bandana.

"For us?"

"They're mine. I plan to retire here, so I'm collecting furniture. You like the oak kitchen table? You could kill a hog on that thing."

"The table is okay. I guess we could use the chairs since we haven't got our own furniture yet."

"That's what I thought," he gestured at his companion and together they unloaded the bulky chairs, pushed them through the entrance and into the living room. I let him, since we would have something to sit on in front of the fireplace. The evenings and mornings were cold and clammy. We hated turning on the air-conditioning units for heat, they spread an awful, dry smell and since Red had provided us with plenty of wood, I kept the fire Mike started at dusk going until the following mid-day. But I had my reservations about a landlord who was so keen on letting me know we were living in his house. So different from the situation in The Netherlands where even rental homes or apartments will be yours, your home, as long as you pay the rent on time.

The weather in the hill country reminded me of the spring storms of my childhood in The Netherlands. Strong winds coming in from the west, bringing mild temperatures. Mike and I helped our friends Leon and Jane, peers of his parents, clear the junk out of their back-yard. Mike made me foreman. The sky was clear, the temperature pleasant, not too warm. With the proper tools, shovel and fork, I felt in my element. Automatically, my hands and body knew what to do.

"Going to town, Judith," Mike laughed out loud, "You sure like yard work don't you?"

I did, even though I had not done any since my childhood. The beauty of the area, the spring in the air was what I had longed for. Nature as healer. The immediate proof of restoration and resurrection always present in the very cycle of life and death.

I got up early, to see ribbons of faint clouds in the pale blue sky escort a sickle of moon out of sight; to hear a scarlet cardinal sing in the budding tree beside the mailbox, to watch the deer retreat in the brush at the far end of our plot.

Mike took the old blue pick-up truck his dad had given us, to work in Austin and I was left without transportation. When his birthday arrived, I could not get to a store, so I drew him a card and presented him with fireplace tools I bought at a garage sale across the street.

"Good for next winter, that is, if we're here," he laughed. "I'd really like to go to Europe at least yearly for a few months."

"That might not be possible for awhile if I get pregnant."

"Having a baby could mean having to put off a lot," he said.

"You want to give me a worse headache? I already woke up with one," I yelled. "Do you, or don't you want a family?"

"Of course I do, but I would like to spend some time with you, just us. I'd like you to experience the summer here without being pregnant. You're already complaining about the temperature and this is only spring."

I saw his explanation as a delay of action. How afraid was he? How much did I want a family? Those days I'd wake up crying, my dreams were made of blood and tears. Mike, Kay and others a blur on my side, with the obstetrician at the foot of the bed, her back turned to me.

What will happen the next time? I wondered. Whom could I rely on in the hill country? What was my problem? Was it not being pregnant? Would the problem be solved by getting pregnant? I knew I needed to talk about my fears and anxiety. If I couldn't find the right people to talk to, I knew I would need to find a counselor. I felt lost. What could I do?

The first time after we made love without protection, I was bewildered by the idea that I could conceive. This notion was immediately connected to the fear of losing this new baby. And therefore the urge or passion, in my mind connected with the making of ARIANE was lacking. I had ambivalent feelings, sometimes good, sometimes terrifying, most of the time unsure.

I needed to talk to a professional about my fears. I remembered Leslie and Beau, a couple we had met through Leon and Jane at a jam session in Wimberley. Leon told me they had five children. Leslie surely would have experience with the local doctors. I looked them up in the phone book and dialed the number. Leslie answered the phone and listened to my request.

"Over here the doctors are all conventional. For female things I go to Anne my midwife. It's a pity she is only a nurse, she can't prescribe anything. Beau and the kids go to the general practitioner in town. Unfortunately doctors here are all fast with prescribing antibiotics. I'm really sorry that my midwife can't write prescriptions."

"What about the dial-a-tune-car doctor?" I asked.

For a moment Leslie was silent, then she burst out in laughter. "That's not a doctor. If you'd call on him, he might wanna look under your hood."

I did not understand, was she joking? "Is he a shrink?"

"No," she roared, "He is a car mechanic."

When I heard that I cracked up too. "I'd like the number of your midwife." After she gave it to me, we laughed some more before ringing off. I called Anne and told her I got her number from Leslie.

"Do you wish to make an appointment?"

"I'm not pregnant."

"Do you wish to wait until you are?" I did not respond. Sensing my discomfort she asked whether I'd like to talk some.

"Right now?" I asked, "I do not wish to impose on you."

"Now is as good as any time, just let me make myself a cup of tea."

Only then did I realize the obnoxious tone in the background was the whistle of the water kettle. When she returned to the phone I told her about our loss, the move and the scary dreams. Anne's response was direct and to the point.

"No matter how much mourning you have done, the grief will always be with you. For the rest of your life. Now that you're thinking about having another baby, the pain, the fear, the anxiety is right there. You'll have to deal with that.

Maybe you've not been aware of your anxiety for awhile, now the fear surfaces in your dreams. You may be helped by keeping a note-book. Write those dreams down. When you keep a record of what scares you, you'll be able to see when and how your fears change. Practically every woman who is pregnant has some fear; for the baby's health as well as for herself. That's normal. Writing down scary dreams will help you confront them in daylight. A bad dream is much scarier during the darkness of the night than during the day."

I could not have agreed more. Having taken care of my immediate need, Anne expressed curiosity about the position of midwives in The Netherlands. While we talked about the differences in health care between the Netherland and the U.S. especially in prenatal care, I stared at the hills in the distance, acutely aware of my loneliness. Communicating with Anne only made more clear that there were no old, or new girlfriends my own age, no familiar doctors, or even the doctor -who owed me one- in close proximity. Our retired neighbors were oddly uninterested in anybody under fifty years of age. Anne's attention made me feel thankful and I told her so.

However, after we rang off, I continued feeling at loss. I wondered who I was, without the comforting reflection found in friends. I wondered where to look for a mirror. Without art to account for my painting, without words on paper to remind me of a work in progress I had to reinvent myself.

I did this by writing about loss, being lost, writing my own self-help book. The Texas sky is great and the horizon wide. While at loss I considered myself rich, unrestricted by expectations, least of all my own. I was eager to open up to possibilities.

Then, Angela of the Austin Writers' League presented me with an honorary membership and two scholarships for a Writers' League workshop weekend. One for a poetry workshop with Bobby Byrd and the other for a fiction workshop with Bobby's wife Lee Merril Byrd. I had wished to go, but couldn't afford to, so I was thrilled. Mike drove me to the campus in the morning and I spent two days with enthusiastic fellow writers. Lee told us how her and Bobby's house burned down. Their two boys were badly hurt by the fire. The incident lead to Lee's writing. Stories from life.

Bobby let us write a poem after Tsang Chih:

᪣᪣᪣

I was brought up in isolation
eager to make contact I smiled hard
passers-by barely nodded
We were weird from the West up North
only the preacher
who wished to convert us dropped by

᪣᪣᪣

Ah, the way writing can bring issues to the surface thinking alone cannot. The poem showed me that I had been homesick for Amsterdam and lonely before, when my parents and I moved away from the city to what was then the isolated northern province of Groningen. As a child I made friends in school, of course. But I spent many a solitary day roaming around meadows, puttering in shallow ditches, building hay bale houses in the barn. Balanced on a branch of an apple tree in the orchard I meditated on adventure stories I had read. Seated on the flat roof of the duck house near the stream in front of our farmhouse, I identified villages at the horizon by the silhouettes of their church steeples. I listened to the grass grow, the barking of dogs in the distance, the buzzing of evening bugs. I practiced walking without a sound. And I read.

I referred to the same in the hill country. Every other day I walked the mile to Old Baldy from our house and climbed the 218 stone steps to the top of the hill. The first time Mike and I went, I reached the top wheezing and scared to descend. I was oblivious to my surroundings, all I saw were the rocks hewn in irregular steps, the dusty dirt in between. As my condition got better the ascent became easier, but I was still afraid to go down on the uneven, rocky steps. Scratchy, dry brush looked uninviting to stumble into. I learned that holding my belly muscles in and my shoulders back helped. My trust in my feet, legs, torso, my whole body, grew and I no longer feared falling down the side of the hill. In the beginning I ascended practically side-ways, after a month of regular exercise

I hopped down the rocky steps with the agility of a mountain goat. I no longer felt exhausted when reaching the top, even after the fourth time up. On the barren cranium of the bushy giant I did my yoga exercises, my feet planted firmly on the dirt; stretching high to greet the sun, spreading wide to reach the horizon, hanging deep to touch the earth.

From there the view of the hill country was unobstructed. Miles and miles of rolling hills covered with live oak and juniper and no apparent manmade structures in sight. The hill country seemed endless, and lonely. Only where Devil's Back-bone and the horizon ran together, the earth and sky met. The only person I saw during those hikes, was a retired colonel, who named each landing of Baldy's steps by an Italian number (he had been stationed in Italy during the Second World War) and who carried doggy treats in his pants pocket to humor the watch dogs he met on his trail, and hard candy he shared with me.

The humid heat soon became unbearable. As long as I left the house by six-thirty I was fine, but I had to be back inside, in the air-conditioned environment before seven-thirty. After that the warm, wet blanket called weather weighed down on me heavily,emphasizing my solitary existence.

Communication with Red was restricted to his furniture offerings and a lesson in creative bookkeeping after I asked him to hold our rent check a couple of days before depositing it.

"Judith, let me explain to you: I use checks as money, I signed your check over to one of my workers on the sixteenth. And he sent it on to his wife in Georgia. I'm telling you it is out of my hands."

Exposure to other poets came in April when I read from my ARIANE chap book at the International Poetry Festival in Austin. The atmosphere was relaxed and congenial. My voice though small, was loud enough and the audience listened attentively. Mikus, the chair of the League's poetry group complimented me, adding that I ought to submit poems for the League's Poetry Anthology. I felt exhausted from reading merely four or five poems and remembered the fifty-minute performance I did in Austin in 1992. But this was the first time I shared poetry about ARIANE with an audience. And I was nervous because of that. I did not talk to anybody beside Mikus and the master of ceremonies, who told me she had enjoyed listening to my reading.

Angela commissioned me to give away books and read at elementary schools. Great fun, I got introduced to American children's books and received a lot of hugs, especially from the little ones.

৯৬ ৯৬ ৯৬

From early on, my urge to write was fueled by the over-powering sense that there might not be a tomorrow. Not that strange a notion, since I grew up with an old, sick father who told me nearly every day that he might be gone the next. This warning concerned more than his own feeble health. Anybody's life can be destroyed, was what he tried to tell me. He proved to me by example that a person lives on, when his or her story is told. He proved so by the books he presented me with. Between age seven and ten, every six months, a package directly from the publisher would be awaiting me, on top of the refrigerator, when I came home for lunch. A children's adventure, like Huckleberry Finn or Tom Sawyer, went accompanied by the newest release in the Sesam series: The Second World War. Only after he had pointed out photographs of war and Holocaust victims; living skeletons staring in the camera, piles of corpses, eye-glasses, gold teeth and smoking chimneys, he would let me go off with the books more suitable for a child my age. My father insisted even grueling stories had to be told and heard; initially my writing was centered around my father's story of loss.

With my pregnancy a sense of future entered my life. Children are the future. My routine of making notes persisted throughout the nine months of pregnancy. After the delivery and loss of our baby daughter, my focus shifted from his-story to her-story or rather my story; my wish to relate my personal experience with loss.

As an immigrant, fresh of the plane, I felt lost in the country I thought I knew so well from previous visits and extended stays. After giving up my apartment in Amsterdam, after selling the electrical appliances as well as most of my art-work and furniture, the material ties with the home-country were severed. With my books, art-supplies and heirlooms packed and on a boat to follow us to our destination, my soul was lost.

I learned on previous occasions that it is not uncommon for body and soul to travel separately. Sometimes my soul comes trailing behind as though unwilling to let go of the known base. Other times, my soul would go ahead and await me at my destination, immediately making me feel welcome and at ease.

This time however, although I had traveled to a familiar place, having left behind friends who witnessed my pregnancy and who had mourned the loss of our baby daughter, made me feel like a zombie, empty and unrecognizable to myself.

I hardly recalled being an artist. In the new environment nobody knew anything about me and I wasn't able to tell strangers more than my foreign sounding name. I had nothing to show. I was still full of my loss, but you don't say to people you meet: "Hi, I am Judith I lost my baby a year ago." Bereft of my child, without a knowing support group, the best I could do was BE and continue.

ଈଈଈ

Seven weeks after we landed, the ship with our container arrived. We retrieved the shipment in Houston. While unpacking and arranging our belongings we came across ARIANE's things.

"The baby clothes," I handed Mike the big vacuum cleaner box packed with forty diapers we got from his brother.

"Our daughter's things," he corrected me wiping tears from his eyes.

I had my spell the next day. When I located Peter Rabbit, our giant, white, bunny rabbit, scruffy looking with his ears folded down in a linen box surrounded by most of his friends, I started crying. After I grouped them in one of the fake rattan chairs Red dropped off, I sprawled out on our bed and told them how glad I was to see all of them.

In my search for birds of a feather, I made contact with another regular of the Wimberley jam sessions, a reporter named Linda. She interviewed me, the new artist in town for The Wimberley newspaper. She looked at my port-folios and noticed the Blood Loss series. "Why Blood loss?" She inquired.

Only then did I tell her about our loss. I urged her not to write about that part of my life in her feature. I was afraid Linda would turn my life into a sob story and I did not want anybody's pity. Months later, I felt I betrayed ARIANE's memory by not wanting Linda to mention our baby's birth and death in the article, I regretted she did not write that I was the mother of a daughter who had died at birth. But I was not familiar with such phrasing at that time.

In May, three months after our arrival, I discovered the phone number of the Pregnancy After Loss Support group of Austin in the back of a local free parenting magazine. A week after talking to Pat, a facilitator of PALS, I received a package with information about grief support groups, a catalog of Wintergreen Press, a copy of *Reproductive Resource Review,* and an article by Betsy Busby, M.Div.: *Grief and Healing Stages of a Pregnancy Loss,* in which she described the four phases of grief. Initial grief is followed by a period of searching and yearning during which the parents are haunted by the unanswerable question "WHY?" Then comes the beginning of acceptance. Fourth and last comes resolution when parents have found a way to incorporate their baby's life and death into the new life they must create for themselves.

In The Netherlands I had found neither reading material nor a support group focused on infant loss. When I asked Carita about us joining the national support group for bereft parents (VOOK), she told me we would not feel at home in the company of parents who had lost older children. I recalled the importance of two pieces of mail we received after ARIANE's birth and death. One a short story concerning the death of a baby, clipped from a newspaper by our friend Spike in America, and the other a magazine article on how Aborigines deal with infant death from Paul in Australia. Getting informed helped me gain perspective in my own situation.

And from Betsy's by-line I learned that she was the mother of one child, Blyth-Ann, who was stillborn.

"I like that, I like thinking of myself as the father of ARIANE," Mike said, after I read the by-line to him. We decided to adopt that phrase. We are the parents of one child, who died at birth.

ॐॐॐ

THE OCEAN

Time washes away the tears,
polishes the hurt until only
smooth scars, the ragged edges
gone, turn up once again
between new patterns drawn
by the tide.

At least twice a week I went to Wimberley's library, making my choice of both fiction and non-fiction from the new acquisitions shelf. *The Healing Brain* by Robert Ornstein and David Sobel was a find. According to the authors, "People with close ties to others maintain a stable view of the world and are able to rely on friends for help and support, thus avoiding the panic, indecision, instability and illness which often accompany major changes in geographic and cultural circumstances.

Social support appears to offer a stability which protects people in times of transition and stress. The perception of good emotional support from families buffer the effects of stress and if a woman was expecting, the pregnancy was not adversely affected by major changes.

We need to understand how social support gets into the body, how our friends communicate with our immune systems, how caring for and being cared for changes our hearts. But part of this seems to involve shifting our attention outside ourselves to the larger group. This shift can occur because of our association with people, pets, or even plants. Communicate with others, bonding, appears to be vital to our health and is deeply rooted in human evolution. Strong attachments have a survival function."

I understood and agreed with this statement. And yet, in July, giving up on the weather and our landlord, we left Texas where I had started to make some friends, for the unknown Pacific Northwest. We put our belongings in storage, packed Old Blue with camping gear and went on our way to Seattle where we were to house-sit for Zack, a son of friends in California. That road trip is stored in my mind as a long distance motion picture starting off with Texas by night and ending in evergreen Washington. Zack had given us detailed directions we needed to follow, or we would get lost, he had stressed on the phone. The Emerald City, sprawled across seven hills, presented herself in all the splendor of a sparkling gem under a blue sky. We saw from the Interstate how inlets and lakes created natural dividers between residential neighborhoods, speckled with plenty of green. Sunlight reflected off water as well as countless windows of high-rises downtown, made for a brilliant sight. We drove around and up Queen Anne hill and found Zack's home as promised, a yellow, craftsman bungalow with a rocker and a cocker spaniel on the front porch. He showed us around and we settled in. Soon after our arrival he departed for a trip to Europe.

All streets in the neighborhood were lined by trees and many back-yard's, like Zack's, were regular orchards with fruit bearing cherry, plum, apple and pear trees. Blackberry bushes graced slopes and deserted lots, a picker's heaven. From some streets we had an unobstructed view of Seattle's bay, the Puget Sound, with islands in the distance that had the Olympic Mountains as a backdrop. On one of my early walks I discovered the nearby cemetery. Situated on top of the hill, it had pleasantly winding pathways and through knotty, branch windows shaped by bushes and beech trees I could see the Cascades in the east.

One day, the week-day walker of Zack's dog Lola came to the front door with a woman he introduced as his wife. We had met him, but only briefly, we had promised Zack to take care of his pooch and that included taking her for walks and a swim.

"We were in the neighborhood and thought we'd wish the big guy a good trip."

"He has left already."

"Oh."

"Would you like to come in?"

The man walked to the couch and sat down. The woman, carrying a baby girl sat down beside him. She looked me over from top to toe.

"Do you have a baby?" she asked.

"We had a baby," I felt my stomach tighten.

🚲🚲🚲

LIFE

She goes to funerals to weep
at the cemetery she cries
for all the dead. But it's
life that brings the
tears stream freely over
the loss of her baby

🚲🚲🚲

Seattle is a livable city, that's what we were told by everybody we met. A heaven for hikers, mountaineers, and people who love water sports and on top of that a haven for creative people. Mike said there was plenty going on in the theater, he considered moving to Seattle for good.

I was willing to believe that Seattle had plenty of possibilities, but I did not see or feel it. Not that I didn't appreciate the scenery, or the activities I read about in the tabloids. I did, but in a removed way. I walked all over town trying to find what would make me tick and all I got was a bump on my Achilles, soft like a blister, but without the fluid inside. At first I refused to let the pain slow me down, I insisted on finding my way around town on foot, I had to make Seattle mine, the way I had Berlin, Palma, Paris, any place I ever lived, even parts of Los Angeles. The bump got bigger and more painful every day. All my life I had run, I was always in a hurry to reach my goals, to accomplish what I wanted. What I wanted out of life then, could not be had quickly. I felt lost, lonely and out of control.

ⱥⱥⱥ

If I think real hard
I may remember
who I am
When and where
did I leave myself behind
Many things I have done
convictions I had
I can remember
Only
When I think real hard
Certain people know me
better than I do
Others see me the way
I am not
All I am is now
The past a memory
which may be traced
but never recovered
Through new life and death
I've found the present

ⱥⱥⱥ

During our first month in the Northwest, we went on an outing to Quinault National Park on the Olympic Peninsula. Under a roof of evergreens and blue sky, I burst out in a litany similar to the one I held at the Burger King in Amsterdam a year earlier.

We had entered the picnic area of the park to have lunch at one of the tables. Neither of us had any idea what set the verbal explosion off. I talked with my mouthful, pushing words out between bites of turkey and cheese sandwich.

"Why didn't you tell the obstetrician all that," Mike snapped.

"Don't give me that voice," I bit back.

"I'm angry too, I hurt as well, we can't bring ARIANE back she is dead." He wasn't crying then, not yet.

"I've got to go for a walk," he got up and took off.

Leaving me bent over the table, determined to finish my sandwich. I remember my nails were dirty, the bread white, the texture dense but not pudgy. An open structure and yet firm. The turkey slices, slightly damp, were crisp to the bite. The Swiss cheese with holes had the familiar open taste which makes Emmenthaler so good to combine with other flavors. Chewing was hard.

Why can't life be easy? I thought. How can life go on when the thin end of the wedge has been driven into my heart. What impulses make the molars roll over and mash and slide and mill food, while all I feel is anger and pain.

I cried my eyes out. When Mike came back from his walk, he talked, looking at me from blue and red, watery eyes. Gems in sockets. Tears rolled down his cheeks. He spoke with urgency, about his grief and how mine seemed to have been enough for the two of us. He had kept his hurt inside; the pain over losing ARIANE.

"I may have shared the loss by telling a close friend, but I never shared my grief; until now, with you."

Finally, after one and a half years of internal mourning.

"I loved ARIANE the whole time she was in your belly. I loved her when we held her, I loved her then and I still do. Nothing will change that," Mike told me after our weeping.

৵৵৵

"Did you have a baby recently?" The hairdresser parted my thinned out curls with a broad tooth comb.

"Yes, a year and a half ago."

"That explains your hair-loss, that is not uncommon after giving birth. I believe women need between one and a half and four years to recover physically. Amazing how much of an attack giving birth is on a woman's body." She separated small tails with the aid of a metal clip. "How old is your baby now?"

"She would have been a year and a half, had she lived. She died at child-birth."

The stylist was quiet. I watched the scissors move around my head, thinking: I hope she won't mess up my hair, now that she is upset. But she stopped cutting all together.

"I had something similar."

"Oh."

"I had a miscarriage."

"Oh?"

"...and after the miscarriage I was told that I couldn't have children. Ever. The cruelty. You see, all the women in my family are small. Five feet, five feet four at the most and here I am with my five feet nine and I am too small internally." She paused looking at me in the mirror: "You must be strong not to let your loss embitter you."

"My husband and I made a conscious decision not to put the blame on anybody, not to play with guilt. You can't do anything about the pain, but you can work on not becoming bitter. They say time heals all wounds, but I don't think that is true. At times everything seems to be all right, but then, suddenly something may remind me of our reality and the hurt is there again."

"Having lost your baby after carrying her for nine months must be harder on you than the miscarriage was on me."

"You were told you could never have children."

She nodded, "Now that I've got married, people ask me when I am going to have children... That is none of their business." She let her scissors fly through my hair again.

♣♣♣

We decided to stay in Seattle and rented a studio apartment on lower Queen Anne. I felt disoriented, dispersed, not sure about my place in the new environment. A regular job would have brought me in contact with people. In this the solitary nature of my occupation worked against me, artists and writers usually work by themselves. That is, until they find likely tuned people to join forces with. Our landlady showed interest in us, but I refused to tell a near stranger like her what was on my mind. Out of despair I called Marjan and Hanna. Neither of them had any idea what my life was like in America, all they understood was that I had made my own bed...

To my mother I lied, "All is well," so as not to upset her.

Having to wait for free-lance work that was hard to come by for a new-comer in town, made Mike restless. So restless that he convinced himself, then me, he had to drive to Texas to collect his guitar, our winter clothes, books, pots and pans and my art supplies. He went to the storage unit and, without looking what was inside, put the largest suitcase in the back of Old Blue. The case turned out to be filled with skimpy, summer clothes, shoes we ought to have thrown away and bundled clothes hangers. After he drove all that way, I still had nothing warm to wear, no art supplies nor the books I had asked for. So I layered the clothes I had, made sketches with my fountain pen and visited the public library. I searched the catalog for books on infant loss and grief. *How To Go On Living After The Death Of A Baby* was a title I thought I ought to have come across sooner, right after we lost ARIANE. Still it is never too late to read something you can relate to.

"If we're going to try to have another baby, I need a doctor," I told Mike, "I need to start a relationship before I go in labor." We chose a family doctor on the hill. In passing his office on foot, I had seen a whole wall with photos of newborns. Mike and I went in for an introductory visit. After we told the doctor our history he took a tissue from the box then handed the container to us.

"If you get pregnant I can take care of you. I would work closely together with an obstetrician/ gynecologist. But you can also start looking for an obstetrician of your liking. If you wish I can have my assistant give the telephone numbers of a few support groups in town."

One of the groups was named P.S. My baby died. I found out P.S. stood for Parent Support, but the initials did not immediately entice me to call. When I did, a metallic sounding voice told me the mail-box was full.

The other number was for The Compassionate Friends. I found out they were meeting every Thursday but only the second Thursday of the month the meetings were held close to our neighborhood, at the Seattle University campus.

"We have people from all different walks of life and we are not only parents of young children, we have an eighty year old man who mourns the death of his grown-up daughter and there is one couple who had a still-born baby," the woman who took my call told me. We went to our first meeting in October. Mike was tense and I nervous as we drove to the campus. Once inside,

Mike got nervous and I let go. We were greeted warmly by Louise, one of the Seattle chapter's leaders. After asking us whether we had lost a boy or a girl, she handed us square plastic sleeves, with pink slips to write ARIANE's name on. We sat down at the conference table.

"I hate doing this," Mike tossed his pen.
I collected my umbrella and coat from the chair next to mine and whispered: "Okay, let's leave."

Louise looked at us sadly. "I expect Sisi and Chuck any moment now, they also lost their baby..," she accompanied us to the door. "It is not unusual to feel uncomfortable the first time," she pleaded.
A man stood in the door opening. He would not budge.

"I'm Chuck," he offered his hand without moving out of the doorway. "And there is my wife Sisi."

"Hi," a young woman popped up next to Mike, she as well offered her hand. "I understand you have lost your baby at child-birth, so did we."
Mike and I looked at each other.

"Let's have a coffee in another room, now that you've come this far," Chuck stepped back into the hallway to let other group members in.

"Yes, if you want you can tell us what happened and if not, we'll just visit for a while and then you can go," Sisi added.

"Is that okay with you honey?" I asked. Mike nodded.

Since there were no empty rooms available, Sisi and I sat down on the lower steps of the stairs in the back of the hallway while the men leaned against the wall opposite us.

"Did you have a boy or a girl," Sisi looked for the badges we were not wearing.

"A girl, ARIANE EIRA," we replied in chorus.
Chuck and Sisi both wore a blue badge with BEAN written in capital letters over the picture of a round faced baby.

Reluctant at first, we told our story of loss. Then Chuck and Sisi told us what happened to them. BEAN was born a year before ARIANE and they had had another baby since, Ziggy, a boy as well. To meet with them was wonderful. What a relief to talk to people who had gone through a similar ordeal. After a while they said they would like to join a sharing group. For us meeting with them had been enough.

"I'm sorry we have to meet this way, but good meeting you nevertheless," Sisi hugged me tightly. That sentence stuck to me, an old phrase got a whole new meaning. We went home pleased with the contacts we had made.

❧❧❧

MYSELF

My self a feather-like coat
protects me from loneliness
I'm warm like a chicken
under its mother's chest
Comforting care provides warmth I need
to be free to go as I please
to meet and mingle
in an effort to find love
within a group of likely tuned individuals
I need to be stable in myself
know my needs and find that niche
that place where I'll feel secure.

❧❧❧

I tried to follow the advice given in the books I read, telling myself to think in an affirmative way, eat the right food, do positive things, exercise. I told myself to take care of my health, see doctors when necessary, communicate with people, have fun, laugh. I was aware of the effect my brain had on my whole well being.

In the evening before I went to sleep, I envisioned something constructive I could do the next day, like making a postage stamp sized drawing of the Puget Sound; I thought of my Dream Family as a realistic possibility rather than always imagining the worst and I thought of my husband with trust and love.

Mike was careful with me, he called on time when he knew he was going to be late, so hysteria wouldn't get the best of me. He showed interest in how my days went and we visited. I appreciated the attention.

We moved from the cramped studio apartment to a one-bedroom apartment on the second floor. When my mother sent money for my birthday, we decided to use it to go to Texas, rent a moving trailer and bring all of our belongings to Seattle.

The *Living After Loss* book made me aware I was still suffering the aftermath of loosing ARIANE and that fear is normal or rather, not abnormal. Some people decide they'll never try to get pregnant again. They decide to adopt.

I knew I had to talk to an obstetrician about my fears before I would ever dare to get pregnant again. Even our compassionate family doctor could not take away my fears.

ॐॐॐ

IN SPIRIT

I stopped counting in the
eighth month. We weren't ready
yet. To receive her we needed more
time. Suddenly, the only one more
month hit me Only two more
weeks at Christmas and the breech
might still turn. One more week
and I had had it with the bike
My carriage started to drift apart
After the calm of the
year's first week the
water broke. A liberating lightness
carried me from there on
So much motion contracted
in a tornado of time, the
inner core still, silent
dressed in a tumultuous storm
She would not, could not
leave me and I died as
much as she did after
nine months of growing
accustomed to the idea,
the abstraction of
MATERIAL LIFE

ॐॐॐ

I devoured an interview in *Synapse* with Penny Simkin, a physical therapist who after delivering four children herself, came to the conclusion that giving birth (in America) could be a whole lot less stressful if only there was more emotional care for the mother and even the father to be. Simkin promoted the involvement of the DOULA (from the Greek word to care for) an intermediary between the pregnant woman and her partner and the medical care-givers; be they doctors and hospital staff or midwives. A DOULA could have been the person beside Mike, Kay and me, able to translate my wish to stop laboring in favor of a Caesarean. What surprised me was that reading the article brought the good memories I had of my pregnancy to the surface. I remembered Carita's classes and how much I looked forward to them. The pleasure of sharing the experience with other pregnant women, the nurturing effect of Carita's advice on all levels.

☙☙☙

When in doubt, walk. And I don't mean when the going gets rough the rough get going. Walking is one of the best refreshers I have ever known. Better than swimming, which I find boring and in an environment with hills, definitely better than riding a bike. The problem in 1994 was that walking had become painful. On my thirty-ninth birthday, after we had returned from Texas, I went to a foot specialist to have him take a look at my Achilles tendon. The X-rays showed nothing abnormal, I had tendinitis caused by deterioration. The only way the tendon could heal was if I would give my feet a rest.

"Don't walk too much and walk only on level ground. Once around the block, no more. Then after a while when the pain gets less, you can work it up, go two blocks, and so on."

The irony was that in trying to stay ahead of everything and everybody, I had been running all my life. My Achilles tendon forced me to slow down, I was bound to a slow gait. Slow motion as a metaphor for evaluation. Another way of making progress.

In the evening I went to my second Compassionate Friends meeting. Mike stayed home after an exhausting day at work. At first I wondered whether I really wanted to fill the evening of my birthday with sorrow, then I decided that at the T.C.F. meetings sorrow is combined with warmth and gratitude towards compassionate people. I was glad I went for I got to meet Ellen, whom I had talked to on the phone six weeks earlier, in person. She gave me a big hug. The group meeting centered around a special holidays panel, six parents shared their experiences of celebrating the holidays without that special loved one. I was glad Sisi was on the panel; all the other parents had clear memories of their children, rituals that already existed, changes to go through. I identified more with Sisi's story, since she had been heavily pregnant with BEAN throughout the

Christmas season, as I had been with ARIANE. For us Christmas and New Year's will always represent the expectancy, the awaiting of the arrival of the babies we lost.

Later we divided into smaller groups and I had a chance to tell my story once again. The compassionate response of the other mothers was heart warming. At the end of the meeting Ellen approached me and gave me a big hug.

"I hear it's your birthday," she breathed warm air onto my neck, she smelled of flowers. "We celebrate your birth today. If it wasn't for you having been born, ARIANE would not have been born and we would not have met."

An illustration with "a note for Mother" in a magazine dating back to the weeks before Mother's Day, reminded me of a pen and ink -cradle- picture with lace pillow cover that I drew for ARIANE back in Amsterdam when I felt upset about not being able to make her bed. I can still make a baby quilt for our little girl, I thought, a memorial quilt we can put on display in our living room.

Mother. I am ARIANE EIRA's mother. That statement does something to me now as it did in 1994 and back in Amsterdam when I had to fill out the forms to apply for financial aid in paying for the cremation bill. A dead baby's legacy.

It is the reflection,
A bright light lost to the stars,
A recognition, an acknowledgment in passing,
It is the breaking of the water, it is the kick in the belly,
It is the weight on the pelvic floor, at New Year's,
Past, present and future, tied in together by a thrust of
chin against bone,
five lost minutes and fate alone.

Mike ran into Morrison, his best friend from college, who had moved to Seattle with his wife Gale in the late eighties. We met with them for breakfast and we had so much fun that they invited us for Thanksgiving. Accidents and coincidences seemed to run our lives. After Mike hit a car while parallel parking Old

Blue, I became friendly with the owner, a bubbly lady, always immaculate in her plaid, pleated skirts and silk blouses. Mary-Jane was her name, she wrote naturopathic columns for a health food magazine, and had a major weakness for chocolate. She didn't mind at all taking me downtown to get a fix at See's candy store.

On each night of Hanukah we lit a tiny candle, in colors little girls like, in the miniature Menorah I bought in a neighborhood store.

⚄⚄⚄

Mike wrote a song. The salutation read: To Mother Judith.

> ARIANE, sweet child at sea
> Faintest maiden with eyes of green
> When life is o'er, I'll come to thee
> Set a course across the sea
>
> There is a child across the sea
> A maiden fair with eyes of green
> With hands so small but fingers long
> What gentle touch and grip so strong.
>
> With skin as soft as the lamb's fleece
> Hair so fine, curls so sweet
> Her body long so she can reach
> Across the sea and come to me.
>
> When my life's o'er, I'll come to thee
> Set a course, sail the seas
> In heaven deep we'll meet again
> And rise above the sun to greet
>
> But for now, I'll think of thee
> The maiden fair with eyes of green
> When life is o'er, I'll come to thee
> We'll sail away across the sea.

In December, we went to The Compassionate Friends' Potluck Candle Light meeting. The conference room was lit by three large candles on a table in the center. One for the mothers, one for the fathers and one for the children. We all held hands while

Ellen read a poem accompanied by New Age music. Next, we all got a chance to go to the center table, light a candle and mention the name of our child or sibling.

"For ARIANE EIRA," Mike and I said, our hands folded around one candle.

After everyone present had a turn, the overhead lights came on and people mingled. Some longtime divorced men and women who had come to honor their dead children, split after the ceremony, their union only temporary.

After I spoke at the sharing group session a young man said: "A lot has been clarified at this meeting. I never knew that an infant who hadn't even lived after the delivery, could have such a big impact on peoples' lives."

The next day at noon Mike left for Texas. He was tired of waiting for work, in Texas he wouldn't have any problem he said, especially not during the holiday season. Of course we had discussed how lonely I would be during his absence, but he insisted on going.

"You can get together with Morrison and Gale and I'm sure Mary-Jane will be there for you."

After I saw him off, I wandered through the apartment. Nothing had changed. Only his wardrobe was emptier. I put the vacuum cleaner in the space he left behind and stuffed a bag with baby clothes in one of his crates cum storage. Way past my lunch time I experienced a sudden drop in blood sugar. A cup of yogurt did nothing. Breathing rapidly, I zapped a yam in the micro-wave for a complex carbohydrate snack. I spooned the orange mush, but the shortness of breath continued. Trembling all over, I feared I would die. Seated on the floor so I couldn't fall any lower, I called my general practitioner's office.

"What are the symptoms?" he asked. I told him.

"Sounds like you're having a panic attack caused by hypoglycemia, combined with anxiety."

"That's what I thought. I have eaten something already..."

"What can I do for you?"

"I would like you to take a look at me, examine me and tell me I am not going to die."

"I can tell you that right now, but if you think it is going to make you feel better if I tell you in person, you can come to the office. I'll transfer you to my assistant and she'll set up a time for you."

I was told I could come over right away. On my way to the bus-stop, I walked even more slowly than I had grown accustomed to, afraid to break down in the street. I boarded the bus and arrived at the practice on the hill without any problems.

A mere look at my face made the receptionist point at a box of tissues on the counter. As I pulled a supply from the container, I noticed the framed photograph of a lovely little girl in a party dress. Her hair was blond and curly and in the picture she was about two years old. I wept. ARIANE would have been that age and I was going to have to celebrate the anniversary of her birthday all by myself. Turning my back to the other people awaiting their appointments, I leaned into the wall, trying to stifle my sobs in the already drenched wad of Kleenex. The receptionist approached me from behind her desk.

"Would you like to be in a room by yourself?" she touched the sleeve of my coat. I nodded, thankful for her understanding. A nurse with a bad-hair-day, stern in a white pant-suit, was less willing to make exceptions.

"The doctor is with a patient," she stared at something beyond me through through giant bifocals.

"Can't you put her in a room by herself?"

The nurse shrugged, then beckoned me to follow her. "You can go in there, the doctor will be with you shortly," she pointed at a door in the back of the corridor. Only a few minutes later the doctor bent his balding head as he stepped into the room. Without work coat, in corduroy pants and a knitted cardigan, he looked even more friendly than I remembered him. He tapped my back to listen to the resonance and felt the tension of the muscles in my back and neck. The touch of his hand felt comforting, reassuring.

"Physically you are in good shape, but you are under a lot of stress and holding on to that in your neck and back. You say you don't want to take anti-depressants, so I suggest you take a warm bath and have a massage," he scribbled something on his prescription pad.

"Lori is a wonderful massage therapist, most sensitive and very good at what she does.Why don't you give her a call," he escorted me through the hallway, "her office is at the foot of the hill, only a couple of blocks from where you live. Good luck."

I breathed easier after talking to my doctor. Anxiety attacks really made me feel lonely. I could have called the help number of The Compassionate Friends, Morrison and Gale, or Mary-Jane, but asking help from people I only knew for such a short time didn't come to my mind at the time.

That evening I baked thirty-three sugarless short-bread balls and dusted them with powdered sugar. Had some of those snow-balls for dessert. I cut off the bottom part of the coffee bags with Christmas decorations I'd been saving, fabricated small candy bags out of the tops and filled each with six snow-balls. I presented my doctor and his assistant with my sweet treat when I went in for a Pap-smear a couple of days later. While he went through the routine, he asked how I had been after the anxiety attack.

"You're depression prone, alone in a strange town, without spouse or friends. I suggest an anti-depressant as an option. Just so you won't fly off the handle. People who are taking the medication I'm thinking off say they hardly notice any difference, but those around them do. They look and act happier."

I told him again I didn't feel I needed an anti-depressant. "I'll first try a massage."

"Think about it," he said.

≈≈≈

I have a clear memory of meeting Lori the massage therapist. Her long slender arms, bare in a short sleeved shirt in the middle of winter, came ahead of her, spread, ready to embrace me. Too fast, too soon. I extended my arm. Respecting my initial need for distance, she shook my hand. Thick black hair barely tamed into a ponytail swung as she moved. I had already talked to her on the phone, but she invited me to sit down on the baroque sofa in her front office to fill out a form. She sat on a matching chair, poised like a dancer, observing me with large brown eyes, curious and careful, but more for me than herself. "How do you feel today, and what would you like me to do for you?" was part of the protocol. Shadow boxes with intriguing collages, small pieces of art and art photographs decorated the walls. Fresh flowers and plants stood on side tables, on the floor in front of the windows and in the sills. Everywhere I looked I saw touches of mindfulness, an open eye, interest in life; a display of pebbles, chocolates in a basket, a pile of black patent-leather dance shoes in children's sizes.

"I've had massages before, I'm not afraid of being touched. If you're ready, so am I," I said. She let me into the back-room and left me alone to undress and get on the table.

"Are you all tucked in and comfy?" She knocked on the door before entering. Gentle hands made acquaintance with my eager body. Fingers tip-toed through the labyrinth of muscle fibers and nerve endings. Through the hole in the face cradle I watched her bare feet, strong feet, grounded on the hardwood floor. She danced around me, searching, following the outline of my shield, probing careful fingertips underneath, lifting, lightening my load.

❧❧❧

On Christmas eve I was hit by a bad head ache. After dinner I took an aspirin. To no avail. An hour later I took a second one. I had cold shivers and donned my heavy, woolen, navy-blue sweater, tied a scarf around my neck and covered myself with my red comfort blanky. Still cold shivers continued to run across my spine. I dozed off nevertheless, drifting between being awake and asleep. Like a cat I snoozed, opening my eyes at different intervals; shows on the television mingled in with dreams, creating a dazzling spectrum of images and sounds, until I finally came to my senses and got up from the couch to go to bed at 4:00 A.M. It wasn't until then, that I recalled Christmas 1992, when I was so scared by the notion that ARIANE was in breech, when I hyper ventilated. My body remembered.

A few days earlier, returning from the store, I had seen ARIANE's face in front of me, as though projected on an invisible screen. A portrait enlarged from one of the photos Kay made for us while we were holding our baby for the first and last time. ARIANE looked pretty and serene. Seeing her like that, brought a screen of tears to my eyes. The image stayed with me.

Mary-Jane invited me for a brunch on Christmas morning and I wound up having dinner with her family as well. Her husband, her brother with his wife and her mother, their little girl, they all made me feel welcome. Being in the company of the three-year-old sent me home with mixed feelings.

❧❧❧

THIS SADNESS

THIS SADNESS IS pink and orange and yellow THIS SADNESS IS dressed up with bows and ribbons THIS SADNESS IS satiny and smooth skinned and curly haired THIS SADNESS IS dancing and jumping rope and being licked in the face by grown-up dogs THIS SADNESS IS bare legs and little sneakers THIS SADNESS IS knit sweaters and wet sheets and Mickey Mouse comforter covers THIS SADNESS IS rosy cheeks and scarves and mittens and learning how to read THIS SADNESS IS stringing beads and cutting Chinese lanterns out of colored paper and trimming the tree THIS SADNESS IS carrots in a clog and sugar candy in return THIS SADNESS IS Sinterklaas and awkward poems and surprise packages of gifts hidden in detergent cartons THIS SADNESS IS lighting tiny Hanukkah candles in little girl's favorite colors THIS SADNESS IS sticky and sweet and dark brown of chocolate covered cheeks and wet smelly kisses that leave their mark THIS SADNESS IS warm and snugly with candy cane stockings and leather soled socks THIS SADNESS IS high pitched screams and whispered secrets in my ear THIS SADNESS IS rubbing noses and telling stories seated on the dining room floor THIS SADNESS IS watching the squirrels and being ticklish and loving to sing THIS SADNESS IS riding horsy on daddy's shoulders and drumming his hat with both hands THIS SADNESS IS talking to strangers and thanking the bus-driver and skipping rope THIS SADNESS IS saying no to sprouts and yes to potatoes and possibly olives THIS SADNESS IS making no a powerful tool THIS SADNESS IS cookie cutters and flour on the floor and spaghetti on the wall THIS SADNESS IS too much laundry and sleepless nights THIS SADNESS IS blowing out candles THIS SADNESS IS one more year added THIS SADNESS IS NEVER ENDING THIS SADNESS IS MINE

⚘⚘⚘

At times I thought about giving the baby clothes away, make a donation to the homeless women and children service. In my mind I would make piles of what to keep and what to give away. I wanted to hold on to what I knitted. I wanted to hold on to the second hand clothes and to the few new pieces I bought. I would end up wanting to hold on to everything. For the next baby.

I thought perhaps we should have dressed ARIANE in the black velvet stirrup pants, they would have fitted her fine, but I knew, what she wore didn't really matter. At any rate, those clothes were hers and I wanted to hold on to them. I imagined them pressed behind glass in a frame. Small black velvet pants, white lace and fields of flowers.

On the phone from Austin, Mike told me he wanted to have another baby. "I have not felt that way since ARIANE was born."

I wished for the same, but often thought: We never have to have another child of our own, we can live together forever, or separate and together.

ই ই ই

That winter, I followed all the suggestions on how to relax, how to be kind to myself. I drew many a bath. Emerald water in the tub. My toes peeking out, pink and soft, baby seals. Looking at my belly, big and fat, I recalled the bath two years earlier in Marjan's bathtub, in anticipation of the mid-wives' attempt to turn our baby. Heartache came and went. No despair, merely a nauseating sadness, rolling over and around in my belly, spiraling up into my throat as a small ache, a low note.

What is this life good for? I mused. What are we here for? Why?

All I knew for sure was that Mike and I needed each other to heal. what really mattered was our growth.

I'll always be thankful for having been able to get that close to somebody, even if we had to break away, in order to heal and grow up. Life, death and rebirth.

Excerpt from a fax I received from Mike during his
    absence:

> This is the birthday of our darling daughter. I
> have been with her for most of the day. I went for
> a long walk in Zilker Park this morning. Somehow
> nature allows me to feel closer to her. Just me and
> her. My heart is with you on this day. Please
> know that I am with you in spirit.

What I wrote back:

> I'm with you in spirit also. And I know ARIANE
> EIRA is with us as well. The past days I felt
> expectant again. Like last year, but different. I've
> had many memories coming to me. Somehow I
> am a little scared to think, really think of the birth

day. I do so nevertheless. I have been trying to be
kind to myself, but feel apathetic. You've made
my day by sending your fax. I went for a walk this
afternoon. At Elliott Bay Bookstore in Pioneer
Square I saw a little girl climbing the interior steps
hands and feet.

"She is thirteen months old," her father
volunteered. She had small blond curls and once
she noticed my gaze, she kept on looking back
at me.

I caught myself thinking: Maybe they all share a
universal soul, these little things, and they all
know us, ARIANE's parents

৵

Starlight

RECOVERY

In February Mike's work took him from Texas to the West Coast, to Los Angeles. I felt relieved. He was coming back my way. I knew we belonged together. I had not wanted to tell him that I needed him. But then he told me.

"You need me," he said, "You need me and I can't do much for you at such a distance. I am so sorry I left you alone for the holidays and the anniversary of ARIANE's birthday. I couldn't deal with the pain. I did not know that at the time. I'll do whatever it takes to be with you. If I can't find work in my trade, I'll do whatever I can get. I love you, you are my wife and I want us to be together. How do you think being without you has been for me, after living with you for three years?"

By the end of February, after having visited with Mike in Los Angeles, I decided to stop going to the Compassionate Friends meetings. I had found solace attending, but at the same time many of the stories related by the bereft parents created additional fear in me. Fear of losing the next baby, maybe as an older child. Fear of getting pregnant again. Fear of life. The day after my decision, I received a package in the mail from Pen Parents. The package included a Lamaze magazine and two issues of the PAILS of Hope (Pregnancy and Parenting After Infertility and/ or Loss Support)newsletter, plus some flyers concerning infant death or advice columns focused on life and continuation. I nestled in our bed with a cup of tea on the night table and got an emotional boost from reading the material. I was able to look forward to life again. The fear of losing a child would always be there. But we were not middle aged parents who had suffered the loss of a grown child. We were still young enough to have another go at biological parenthood. That notion made me feel jubilant.

PAILS of Hope provided me with buckets of prospects. No longer only the fear of losing a child, but hope. Hope to conceive, hope to deliver, hope to raise.

I called Ellen of The Compassionate Friends and told her about PAILS and why I wouldn't be coming to T.C.F. meetings in the future.

"I understand. Did you ever go to a P.S. My Baby Died meeting?"

I told her their voice mail box had been full every time I called. "That's terrible. I'll try to get in touch with them and if I get a hold of somebody I'll tell them they've got to do something about that. Don't you give up on them, I do wish you would try again."

The next time I tried, I did get through. I left a message and my call was returned by a facilitator named Leah. She told me she had a seven-week-old baby boy and last December had been the first anniversary of her son Peter's birth and death. He was in breech as well, which was not detected until full dilation had taken place. We talked until her baby started fussing.

"Why don't you come to the next meeting on the second of March. I'll fetch you," she offered, knowing that I was without transportation. "Sure," I said, "Why not."

Unfamiliar with the west-side street plan Leah was late picking me up and when we arrived at Children's Hospital, another facilitator had already started the group session. We found a seat in the circle. When the woman who was speaking had finished her sad story about a recent miscarriage, Leah, sighing, looked around for familiar faces.

"How have you been since the last time we saw each other?" She addressed a thirty-something couple seated to the left of me. The woman, crumbling a Kleenex in her hands, bent her head while her partner spoke.

"Dinah is still afraid to get pregnant after the tragic loss of our first baby," he took off his steamy glasses to wipe them with a cloth he pulled from his vest pocket.

A pang of recognition made me cringe.

"He doesn't understand," the wife, a timid smile on her face looked up at us.

"You are new here," the male facilitator seeing my reaction, nodded at me, "My name is David, would you like to say something about Greg and Dinah's issue and perhaps share your own story with the group?"

After I introduced myself, I told the others our story and where I was in it. Tears welled as I talked about the delivery.

"I relate to Dinah's fear to get pregnant again. My next step will be to find a doctor I can trust who will be there for me while I'm pregnant and during the delivery."

When I finished, a man across the room from me said he was surprised and shocked to hear that two years after the loss of our babies we (for Leah had also made remarks along those lines), seemed to still be suffering from our loss in some way or other. He and his wife were the freshest bereft parents. She only delivered their baby ten days earlier. I recognized the way she held her hand protectively on her belly, as well as their collected behavior.

"They were still in shock," Leah said afterwards, "I remember being numb, don't you?"

Within the support group, it was easy to recognize the different stages of grief. To listen to others helped me acknowledge what we had gone through already and to get a clearer idea of where we were ourselves.

An important difference for me between P.S. and The Compassionate Friends, was indeed the fact that P.S. is for people who lost their babies as infants, or stillborn, or due to miscarriage, where as T.C.F. attracts mostly parents who have lost an older child.

The logo of The Compassionate Friends is a butterfly. When I found at least sixty brass butterflies with a wingspan of an inch and a half at the moving sale of an interior decorator, I bought them all, convinced I would find a good use for them.

I made a -sweet dreams- lavender sachet in the shape of a heart for Mike's birthday. After cutting the shape out of the finest Liberty of London cotton, the print resembling a field of corn flowers and poppies, I gave it body with polyester fiber and lavender. Next I made a blanket stitch all around the heart. Then using those stitches to hook into, I crocheted a lacy border with embroidery floss in mixed blue hues. In the middle, slightly off center I fastened a brass butterfly with floss and two translucent beads, like tears of dew on the butterfly's body. At the lowest point of the heart, I attached a blue tassel, working a third bead nearly hidden in the knot. It was relaxing to work on the sachets. I kept on thinking about ARIANE our sweet heart.

The next heart I made was for Mama's birthday. Working with lavender in the evening made me sleep like a rose.

Browsing through the books on the new acquisitions shelf at Queen Anne library, I found *Our Children Forever,* a report on medium George Anderson's psychic sessions with children who have passed on. I started crying while scanning the book's content and checked it out. After I read the whole book I saw ARIANE as our lovely sweet lightness. Her Lightness, Her Sweet Being.

&&&

Lori called me Turtle Woman, a person with a soft sensitive body and a many faceted shield on her back. Each facet holding a story. While massaging my back, she could touch a trigger point that would unleash an anecdote. Words rolled out of my mouth forming a tale she enjoyed listening to, and I enjoyed telling. One time, a Darth Vader quality of darkness and the unknown came to the surface. We both felt a jolt of energy.

"Part of your turtle shield," Lori collected herself and continued.

Then, one day, before our session, she presented me with a small wooden turtle from Africa, painted black and yellow with white lines on the shield. A turtle wearing a dotted body stocking.

&&&

By the beginning of April Mike returned to Seattle. With the help of our general practitioner we found an obstetrician.

"I have somebody in mind whom people either love or hate, I think you'll love her," he said when we asked for suggestions.

He was correct. I had made a check list of questions she would have to answer for us in a satisfying manner. She did more than that, she took away my unreasonable fears.

"How much did you weigh at birth? Five hundred grams? Well then your ARIANE was only fifty grams, an ounce and a half, lighter than you. And no, your baby's death was not your fault, your baby should have been born by C-section. Here, doctors would have had you in the operation room in no time.

Your placenta too small? I don't think so, not in comparison to your baby. You are a healthy woman; you are a healthy couple; your chromosomes are in order. You're only forty, you have a good chance to have another baby."

On my third Mother's Day, I laid out a memorial baby quilt. A colorful field of one-inch patches with tiny flowers, silver lame and satin. Months later, when the memorial quilt was finished, I embroidered "ARIANE EIRA, born in Amsterdam on January 8 1993 to Mike and Judith" on the back.

❧❧❧

After ARIANE passed on, when I wanted to make Art with a capital A, I struggled to come up with something clever. But I discovered the simplest of ideas were the most effective. In Texas I found myself at a deadlock. Nothing worthwhile seemed to come out of my hands, but at least I worked on my own self-help book and I enjoyed the healing force of nature. In Seattle, without Mike, I started to make colorful drawings, studies from life, which I sent to him.

Building ARIANE's lavender hearts worked like therapy. And the people I'd present with one, cherished my tokens of love for their pure sweetness; the soothing effect of sweet, lavender induced dreams. I learned to take care of myself, how to be a whole-some-body and that simple pleasures are the best. I learned that you can help people by actively listening, that is, to ask a difficult question sometimes. I learned that the pain of loss eases, and that the Lightness is there, only a level away, surrounding us, mixed in with sunshine, the light of the stars.

Sunshine, starlight, sunlight, starshine.

❧

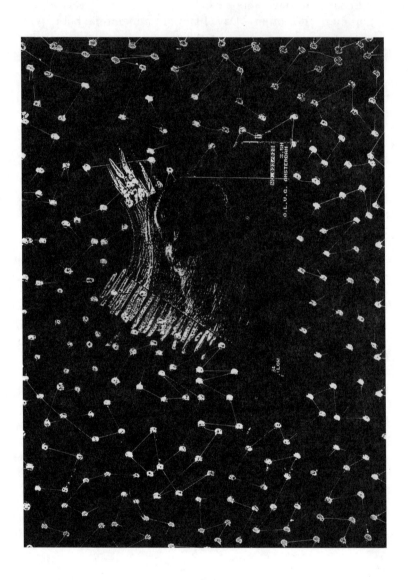

Galaxy

EPILOGUE

Writing this book was my number one creative activity during the past five years, reading undoubtedly number two. At the time of our loss and the first year thereafter, I could not find enough to read on the subject of infant loss. Knowing that you are not the only one, that there are others who have gone through a similar ordeal is of the utmost importance after a tragedy has occurred. Not merely to help you identify, but also to help you understand that the situation, however dark, will change. At first I waited for stories to come my way. And indeed some friends sent a poem, a story, an article, or shared experiences of their own. But I wanted more. I wanted to know what I could expect, whether there would be light at the end of the tunnel. Once I found out about support groups, I sent for their brochures or news letters and through those I discovered university and specialty presses like Wintergreen that offered the much needed material. Internet access has opened a world of possibilities. Support groups, library catalogs, pen pals and old friends have come within reach of even those in the most remote areas of the world. If writing your own self help book seems too large an endeavor, you can start by connecting with other bereaved parents through the Internet. As the first line of the The Compassionate Friends credo tells us: we need not walk alone.

WORLD WIDE WEB CHILD LOSS PAGES

HYGEIA

http://www.hygeia.org/preface.htm. is an online magazine facilitated by Michael Berman, M.D. Besides offering a platform for poetry and prose, this site provides countless links, references and resources. Hygeia also hosts a chat group.

THE COMPASSIONATE FRIENDS

http://compassionatefriends.com has nearly 600 chapters in the U.S. with regular meetings.

MINING COMPANY

http://pregnancy.miningco.com/msub18.htm

PEN PARENTS http://www.penparents.org
provides pen pals who have suffered similar losses.

SPALS http://www.inforamp.net/~bfo/spals
provides support during subsequent pregnancies.

NATIONAL SHARE OFFICE

http://www.NationalSHAREOffice.com

WORLD WIDE WEB GRIEF PAGES

http://www.webhealing.com/wwwboard

Virtual Memorials
http://www.virtual-memorials.com

Virtual Heaven
http://www.cyberspace.com/~ais/vhmain.html

Perpetual Memorials
http://www.memorials.com

World Gardens'Virtual Cemetery
http://www.worldgardens.com

Cybermourn
http://www.skc,com/Cybermourn/preview.html

The Funeral Service Center
http://www.funeral.com

Yahoo's Grief Related Index
http://www.yahoo.com/Society_and_Culture/death

Webster's Death Dying and Grief Guide
http://www.katsden.com.death/index.html

World Wide Cemetery
http://www.interlog.com/~cemetery

National Public Radio
http://www.npr.org/programs/death/ End of Life series
with interesting round table discussions

SUGGESTED READING

Finkbeiner, Ann K., *After the Death of a Child*:
Free Press.

Davis, Deborah L. *Empty Cradle, Broken Heart.*
Fulcrum Publishers.

Fritsch, Julie & Sherokee Ilse. *The Anguish of Loss.*
Wintergreen Press.

Kluger-Bell, Kim. *Unspeakable Losses.*
W.W. Norton & Company.

Levang, Elizabeth & Sherokee Ilse *Remembering with Love.*
Fairview Press.

Mehren, Elizabeth & Kushner, Harold. *After the Darkest
Hour the Sun will shine Again.* Fireside.

Ornstein, Robert & Sobel, David. *The Healing Brain:
Breakthrough Discoveries About How The Brain Keeps Us
Healthy.* Simon & Schuster.

From the same authors: *The Healthy Mind, Healthy Body
Handbook.book.*

Rosof, Barbara D. *The Worst Loss.* Henry Holt.

Sarnoff Schiff, Harriet. *The Bereaved Parent.* Viking Press.

Schwiebert, Pat & Kirk, David *When Hello Means Goodbye.*

Sherokee Ilse, *Empty Arms.* Wintergreen Press.

Whitmore Hickman, Martha. *Healing after Loss*: Daily
meditations for working through grief. Avon Books.

Peppers, Larry G. & Knapp, Ronald *How To Go On Living
After The Death Of A Baby.* Peachtree Publishers

INDEX

COLOPHON

This book was designed by Terence Clark and Judith van Praag, set into type by Terence Clark at small print graphics in Seattle, Washington, and printed and bound by Gorham Printing in Rochester, Washington.

The typeface is Palamino, issued in digital form by Softkey/TLC Cambridge, Massachusetts.

The paper: for the text is 60 lb. Exact Opaque natural, and for the cover, 10pt. white Caroline C1S.